WALKING A MILE IN YOUR SHOES:

My Spiritual Journey with Lucky Dube

By Lenah Mochoele

COPYRIGHT

Words and Music by Lucky Dube

© 1993 – Administered by Gallo Music Publishers

"Prisoner"

Words and Music by Lucky Dube

© 1989 – Administered by Gallo Music Publishers

CONTENTS

WALKING A MILE IN YOUR SHOES: 1

COPYRIGHT 2

CONTENTS 4

PREFACE 8

1. LUCKY'S STORY – MY VERSION 17

2. HIS ESSENCE 25

3. PURPOSE-DRIVEN LIFE 75

4. AN ADVOCATE OF ORDER 97

5. A TRUE AFRICAN HERO 103

6. HIS CAREER 133

7. THE LEGACY 137

8. LIFE TOO SHORT? 145

9. LUCKY DIES 153

10. THE COURT CASE 195

11. REMEMBERING YOU 201

EPILOGUE 211

ABOUT THE AUTHOR 217

ACKNOWLEDGEMENTS

Jehovah Shammah You Who were present, You who are present, You who will be present until the end of time, I thank you, Lord for the wisdom, I thank you Lord for the strength you gave me all the time. When I was too lazy to write you woke me up in the middle of the night and planted that idea I needed for the book. Although I was grumpy you gave me the energy and will to just do it!

Jehovah Jireh You that provided everything I needed, the resources sometimes in the form of friends, the challenges, the gift of writing, I thank you Lord for it all.

Jehovah Shalom You Who are peace, thank you for the peace you provided throughout my journey, when I was disturbed you said be still, when I was afraid you said be still, thank you Lord for the peace even through the rivers of tears I shed during this journey.

Jehovah Rohi You are my shepherd, thank you for dealing with the fear, the doubts, the low self esteem. I thank you Lord for the assurance that when I have you I have everything I need, thank you because everything is possible through You who strengthens me.

I thank you Lord in all Your forms.

I thank my beautiful daughters, Koketso, Puseletso and Kamano. When I locked myself in my bedroom asking not to be disturbed I thank you for understanding, I have never loved you less. You are the reason I can afford a smile each day. Ms Kamano "my editor in chief," thanks my Angel, you've done a great job.

I will forever be indebted to Lucky's family. Thank you for the continued friendship, life has to go on.

Thank you Ma'Mdluli for opening up to me whenever you were troubled; I am still here if you need me. Thank you for the update on the boys, thank you for just being you, young beautiful and strong!

Sibongile, now I have to tell you that you are beautiful and stubborn – the two traits that you made sure you inherited from your father.

Nkulee the sky is the limit for you, baby girl. Your encounter with Dad was short but that should be an advantage that no one can steal from you, stay blessed.

Thokozani, I have no words for you, I will have to write another book to cover everything ... you are my tiger, Mtima, Mazombe, Masbekela, wena o lusa nge Mercedez Benz!

To Laura, I am still figuring out the connection between you and me, baby, but just know that Daddy loved you too much, you were his little princess.

To the young ones, Siyanda, Philani and Melokhuhle– grow up to be responsible, remain blessed, you are sons of the soil, the Lord God of your father will provide for all your needs.

To sis Thandi, Pat and to the whole Dube family, I am humbled to have known you although during a very difficult time – may God bless all of you.

Sis Dudu Khoza, you have shown me that your friendship with Lucky was genuine, you have inspired me in a way you would never understand, thanks for being there for Lucky's family. Thank you for your straight, no-nonsense personality – know that Lucky's family will need you, kuze kuse!

Dave Segal, thank you for your continued support for Lucky's legacy, thank you for being there as a source that I draw strength from, thank you Rabbi!

The Lucky Dube band, I love you. I love you for loving Lucky so much that you would stop at nothing to keep his spirit alive. Bless up!

God bless you my spiritual sister, Nikiwe Thwala (Mbau), you are my rock, thanks sis for being there. You are an amazing friend

God bless you Derick Banjo, my brother from another mother, thank you for the resources from across the sea. I will forever be grateful for what you have done for me; thanks for introducing me to your beautiful family in Paramaribo, Suriname and opening your world to me!

God bless you Glen Gordon Davis, my earthly angel, I am because you are!

Thank you Kim Garbade my sister friend, thank you for all the cat stories, they kept me strong! Be careful Lilly doesn't eat your jump suite…

God bless you, Bau Stone, my brother from the other side, thank you for the resources from across the oceans! Thank you for representing your beloved motherland South Africa in the diaspora, you are truly Proudly South African !

God bless you Lebo M, my brother, friend, Joe, you inspire me! – thank you for the resources through the Lebo M Foundation, much appreciated!

God bless you Sipho Sithole, my brother, thank you for all that you've done for a sister, I appreciate, I am humbled!

To everyone who has contributed to this book – I cannot mention everyone and this does not mean you are any less important – I thank you.

Lucky Dube, thanks for letting me into your life and trusting that I could be a good part of your private space and share your life's journey, it meant the world to me. Sleep well, my Rasta, till we meet again.

PREFACE

The story of Lucky Dube represents a moment in our socio-economic history, humbling, pleasurable and a painful occasion but remains our rich past.

His edu-tainment messages through the litany of his songs still reverberate throughout every corridor of our households, our dusty streets and throughout every length and breadth of our country and beyond.

The world adored and admired him, respected and honored him. The world continues to do so years after his passing on. Lucky Dube's music continues to promote peace and harmony, in the cultural, economic, political and religious tolerance amongst nations in his lifetime and in his death. He'd always become the goodwill ambassador of peace-loving mankind. It is a known fact that Lucky Dube was always venerated by the international community and least celebrated by the country of his forefathers, however, ordinary fellow South Africans loved and valued this giant of a citizen of our land. His music which carries very strong messages has helped us become one with freedom loving people of the world.

I am by my own estimation the luckiest person in the world to have had the privilege to work with this giant who believed we could rise above it all if we were to change the way we were trained to think and strive to work towards being together as one. We can strive to muster the courage to step beyond our comfort zones to contribute towards the progressive mankind the world over. He believed that either through adversity or providence we could change the world we live in to be a better place for the sake of our children and their children's children, a place where each one of us understand that there is more to life than the daily rush. Where fulfilling however the smallest or grandest aspirations would be much more than a fantasy.

I, like the rest of the millions who continue to adore Lucky have one thing in common we understand why he was determined to play his part to change the world so everyone in it could be treated equal, with respect. He empowered those who cared to listen to his music to continue to strive to discern, to always look for the truth. He shared his own life stories through his music, Lucky, like most of us made many mistakes, he allowed himself to be compromised at times, but Lucky knew where he came from. He continued to sing a song of peace and truth albeit knowing he was risking rejection from his own, I believe Lucky accomplished exactly what he had set out to achieve, he saved lives, he left an indelible mark and set the mentally enslaved free.

When Lucky fell I took for myself one special gift that I've drawn strength from, a gift that forms the basis of this book, a gift I would like to share to assist those that still battle with the ability to decide between truth and error in the ever changing patterns of our economic, social, religious, political and cultural changes. That gift is found in the word **discernment.** Wikipedia, a free Encyclopedia defines discernment as: The ability to obtain sharp perceptions or to judge well (or the activity of so doing). In the case of judgement, discernment can be psychological or moral in nature. In the sphere of judgement, discernment involves going past the mere perception of something and making nuanced judgments about its properties or qualities. Considered as a virtue, a discerning individual is considered to possess wisdom, and be of good judgement; especially so with regard to subject matter often overlooked by others.

In its simplest definition, *discernment* is nothing more than the ability to decide between truth and error, right and wrong. *Discernment* is the process of making careful distinctions in our thinking about truth.

I am encouraged by what I learnt during this beautiful journey in the life and times of Lucky Dube who overcame a less than humble beginning to continue to share with others, that no matter how degrading his earlier life was, with determination he stretched beyond his life's barriers to better himself. Lucky maintained his determination and courage that paved the way not only for himself, but for those around him during the course of his life's journey. Though he did not enjoy a perfect childhood it was his courage that propelled him to lead a productive life, he continued day in and day out to make an impact in the world. To encourage others to always stand for the truth, to confront our situations, take charge of our situations and stop believing anything we are told by those that are in authority. Discernment is the message I am conveying in every word of every paragraph in this book. This is how I feel I should share with you the reader of this book, that now more than ever we need to raise future Lucky Dube's, people who will help shape the future of many generations to come . People who will know who they are, do what needs to be done and say it like it is. The Lucky Dube's who will encourage others to lead purpose driven lives from where you are sitting, whether you are good at making tea for a living, cleaning lavatories or doing garden work all of us are as important in doing what truly matters.

I hope when you finish reading this humbling story, you will sit down, look at yourself in the mirror to reflect where you're at in this stage of your life, to truly see yourself without pretence or delusional fantasies that we are forever caught up in. To think about the children and know that the decisions we make today will affect our children and their children's children. These are ever changing times and if we lose the grip to teach the children that life is sacred, if purposely lived it is a precious gift with many promises, then we would have failed to play our roles in shaping the future for them. In these ever changing times we risk losing the opportunity of teaching them that life is more than how much material things you can acquire, lest they grow up thinking life is about chasing after material things with no concern or responsibility for how they would get all of these things. Everyone seems to want to give their children that which they never enjoyed in their childhoods, the best, we seem to want to have children who look at life in rose colored glasses, losing the very lesson that they need to take a stand for their convictions, to lead and make an impact from where they are. There is absolutely nothing wrong in leading a good life, as long as that life fulfils one's purpose to contribute towards humanity. Teach them that our situations may be different we were not born with equal opportunities, that it is not a requirement to have experienced a perfect childhood to make an impact in life. Teach them to know who they are, why they should do the things they should and above all to have faith in their life's missions. I love sharing this simple illustration, that today we live in a world of high technology and I sit and think that if the person that came before me had this grand idea of coming up with inventing computers, what will my contribution be? What will my claim be for occupying space and breathing fresh air all my life? If at this point in my life I battle with this, what about my children and their children's children? Discern precious you, take a stand for your conviction, discern and pave the way that will lead to future generations passing these essential values that are so imperative in shaping our world to generations after them.

Lucky Dube was a proud African man, he played his part in motivating others, I hope sharing his life's story will help you discover a conviction you didn't realize you always had. We are constantly being reminded by South Africans and the progressive mankind the world over, that we have an unfinished business pertaining to Lucky's legacy, that there are so many lessons we can take from what he has left for mankind, and that history shall never absolve us should we fail to recompense in matters of heritage, here is to you the reader of this book, the life and times of Lucky Dube presented through a lens that gives you an insight into why the singer, composer, producer's music dwelt on the suffering and the plight of the poor, against human rights abuse, as part of his chosen subjects.

I have inherited from Lucky the courage to embrace my culture, I am passing this on to the next generation, so they will know who we are, where we come from so they can use this light to show them the way forward. While our traditions are not recognized as sources of substance regardless of the rich wisdom they represent, we should strive to instill our culture in the young ones for culture represents responsibility.

Discern, dig a little deeper, harness the desire to make a change, refuse to bend to the prevailing false promises, don't just be an observer, be the rescuer to the trapped for the sake of our children and their children's children. Discern. God bless you.

His first song (poem)

Oh what a day, a day it was

When my hero sang his first song

Gasping for divine air

To prepare to sing his first song

Oh what a day it was

As Spring was just about

To kiss Winter a goodbye

The African oxygen hurriedly

Occupied space and settled

An African star is born

Oh what a day it was

The divine oxygen settled into one

Divine little body

Oh what a day it was

When the divine oxygen manifested into

Rhythms of divine promises

Promises that

If you hurriedly breath

In and out, in and out

In and out

And in and out

This will be your first divine song

In and out, In and out he breathed

And got his first song

From the top of his voice

With panic broke a divine voice

With divine speed he was breathing

Keeping the rhythm for his first song

Singing so hard the African skies danced

Singing so hard the world stopped and listened

At first thinking it was the cry of a baby

With eager the world listened

Carefully in their multitudes they listened

To confirm if this was indeed a baby's cry

As the world listened to the rhythm of his voice

You sang your first song

At the top of your voice you sang

From their hearts the world listened

An African star was born

Oh what a day, a day it was

When the world embraced a little life

Singing along the rhythm, oh what a day

A day you sang your first song

On a stage you went with inspiration

Not knowing the stage is full of surprises

You sang your song nevertheless

With a voice of Spring

Your first song of Joy the first day

Pain and suffering the next

Future and Promises the day after that

Triumph and tragedy on the last

I remember that day very well

It was that day in 1964

In the month of August

The day was the 3rd

You sang your first song

In the arms of mama Sarah

You sang your first song

Blessed woman she was that day

When you sang your first song

An African Star was born

1. LUCKY'S STORY – MY VERSION

Have you ever wondered why some mothers call their children 'Lucky'? Is it because they're sure they're going to have a charmed life, or is it to give them an advantage, warding off any ill omens by giving them a serendipitous name? They say a rose by any other name would smell as sweet, but if I hear 'thistle' it immediately brings prickly things to mind.

Lucky Dube was many things to many people. To some, he was a father, brother, husband, uncle, prophet and entertainer, while to others he was just 'Sam'. In short, that sums up who Lucky Dube was. He had no power to change his past but he had the gift to influence his future. He grew up with every possible odd you can find in the book stacked against him.

His mother, Sarah, called him Lucky because she had had a number of failed pregnancies before his birth. She and his father separated before he was born, so he was raised by his grandmother whom he adored; she was everything to him. In later life, he referred to her as "his greatest love, the person who made him into the responsible individual he became." Sarah had to go to the big city of Johannesburg to look for a job to be able to fend for her children. Lucky was the third child and the first boy in his family.

He had to start working very early in his life to assist his grandmother to support his other siblings. He started off as a gardener, but soon realised that he wasn't earning enough money and he knew he had to get an education. He had to deal with hunger, poverty, injustice and abuse at an age when children should be receiving love and protection. None of these disadvantages blinded his longing for an education. There was no male role model in his life, but this didn't push him to join the discouraged masses. He

17

walked long distances barefoot to school every day, not complaining about being hungry or tired or cold. He had the courage to deal with his circumstances instead of being overwhelmed by his situation. He was determined to move on to better his life.

One day as he walked back from school feeling very hungry, he picked up an orange peel and ate it. Towards the end of it he took a closer look and saw that there was blood on it. But hunger made him eat it anyway. He told me this story in 2003 when we were in Freetown, Sierra Leone, on a tour.

He asked me, "Rasta," (as Rastafarians we called one another Rasta) "what would you do when you realised that what you'd just swallowed was full of blood?"

My eyes were all teary and I couldn't answer. I suddenly felt sick to my stomach. He said "no, it's okay… I'm not telling you this because I want you to feel sorry for me, but this is what happened."

I remember growing up as a young girl; we also ate orange peels sometimes, but it would be from the orange that you'd just eaten, not those that were picked up from the road.

He told me that walking to and from school was a very interesting journey.

"You're not only looking forward to school or home, you're always on the lookout, hoping that someone driving past would drop a plastic bag with bread and chips or a piece of anything edible," he said. "So you really want to be the first to walk to school or from school for the day's catch. Sometimes if you were lucky you would pick up a bottle of cold drink which you could resell and buy something to eat. An empty stomach is a painful thing ...."

As a child, he was always wondering when his mother would come back home from the big city, which sadly didn't happen for a very long time. He started asking his grandmother every time he saw an unknown female if this was perhaps not his mother. She'd been gone for so long that he was afraid he wouldn't remember her when she showed up. He asked so many times that he eventually gave up asking.

But then came the day when his mother did come home! He felt strange meeting her after all that time, but he was grateful to finally meet his own mother face to face again.

He got on with his life, which was tough. The white people he worked for abused him physically and emotionally but he didn't complain; all he wanted was the bread or the few cents that he'd worked for so that his grandmother and sisters could have something to eat. He didn't give up, hoping that one day his situation would change. He enjoyed going to school and was a bright student too. He particularly loved singing in the school choir; then, already, he realised he had a special talent and he pressed on.

His love for singing became his obsession, helping him rise above the storms of his painful childhood. With some friends in high school, he formed his first ever musical ensemble, The Skyward Band. His love for singing and the realisation that music was his calling – or what others call vocation – made him who he was. His love of music kept him centred and he was inspired by it. He was able to move beyond his life's challenges, knowing that, each day he went to school, he had something to look forward to – his school choir.

* * *

Today I believe that, like He did with many other people in the Bible, God uses what we have in our hands now. He prefers to use existing stuff to turn our situations from nothing to great things. But you have to have something that God can work with, to start off with! There was a lot that Lucky Dube had. There was his passion for music plus his voice; he had a brain; he had humour, charm, and, how can I forget – he had the looks! He was a perfect package from

19

Heaven. There are many examples we read of in the Bible, of people who were not perfect, who did not come from perfect situations. But those very situations were turned around

by God. Think of people like Moses, Joseph and David ... they are perfect examples of God's mercy and unconditional love and favour. When you are favoured by God, your bad situation turns around and becomes your greatest advantage in life. God operates outside of the system that we humans can understand, but there has to be something – a passion, an urge, commitment, love for something – that God can work with.

When he started his career, Lucky didn't think he would become so great and respected, honoured and loved by so many around the world. He was singing simply because he loved singing; he sang from the heart and was passionate about it.

There were many other things he was passionate about: his values; the way he treated others – never once did he forget where he came from. He never pretended that he came from the perfect home. No matter how difficult his childhood was, he never once referred to it as a dark past; he always understood that it was part of his life'sjourney. He knew all about poverty and confronted it head on. He looked straight into its ugly face and poverty was afraid of him, slinking away like a dog with its tail between its legs. How could it do anything but leave when Lucky sang loud, beautiful notes at the top of his voice?

When he stepped beyond the narrow limits of his adverse situation, he stepped up with conviction. The conviction that no matter how difficult his situation, there was always an opportunity for him to become a better person. If the teachers at his school had managed to become teachers, he realised that life couldn't be all that bad. His inner conviction was that if he could endure the worst of all times, as he did, then he might just as well step up and take charge of his life. He believed that there was a better life than the one he'd been subjected to because of South African apartheid.

Just like many others who came before him, Lucky believed in a South Africa where black and white could live together in harmony, without blacks being dependent on whites for survival. He believed that the only way that black people would be free from oppression and inequality was to change the way they had been trained to think. He wanted them to think for themselves and to stop depending on others as if they didn't have the same brains and intellectual capacity.

Lucky's life experience helped him to help others with his message of hope. He told them that things never remain the same if we strive to be better and believe in the gifts that God has given us. "There's always a turning point in all of our lives; it doesn't matter how devastating your situation or circumstance, God will always meet us at our points of need," he said. "The truth about life is that no one knows what tomorrow holds for us, but if we all strive to be better people and live our lives with a true purpose, God will be there for us."

He made me give deep thought to various stories in the Bible. When we dissected the story of the children of Israel and the Promised Land, I remembered that God had put giants to occupy that land, which seemed at first quite strange. But when I thought about it, I saw that these giants were there for a reason – to protect God's interest. Imagine if all the children of Israel had given up on their journey! They would have lost out on the greatest land of that time, the amazing, prosperous land of milk and honey. Lucky told me that, just like the children of Israel, sometimes God protects our blessings with giants in our lives.

When we had these discussions I would simply ask him if he thought God wanted him to walk to school barefoot and on an empty stomach, so that his situation could turn out the way that it did. "What about those individuals whose life situations are not as bad as yours?" I asked. "Why should it be that bad for you? Why not a little bad, why the extreme bad?" He would simply reply, "The situations in our lives are under God's control. It doesn't matter how

21

bad your situation looks, there's always a turning point, always. We were created different for different calls and situations."

People give up too soon, generally speaking. If we pressed on a little more we would realise that there is much more to life than we can see. Lucky loved saying that we give too much power to others, whether it be friends, teachers or politicians. So-called friends will always mislead you, especially when they realise that you're better than they are; teachers will tell you how bad you are at this or that subject, but don't encourage you by saying which ones you're good at; and, of course, politicians will always hide the truth about situations. Lucky would always say that people are complacent; we are comfortable when others validate how good we are but we are unable to acknowledge our own talents and abilities.

Giants in our lives today show as challenges in all areas of our lives. We are poor, we are sick, we are unemployed, albeit highly educated; we are ignorant, we are depressed and we worry constantly about yesterday and tomorrow. We're unable to break through our challenges because we're dependent on others to think for us, to decide who we should be and how we should behave.

Lucky's beliefs have always been amazing to me, so amazing that I've wondered how, with what he achieved over the years, he still gave a damn about what happened around him. His wish was that our leaders would have good ethics and strong convictions about who they are and what they stood for. He wished that they would never forget where they'd come from or the price the whole nation had to pay for them to be where they are now. Some of them have endured really hard times and overcome obstacles we may never understand in the quest to achieve the scrapping of the apartheid system, but if we're not careful all that will have been in vain. What a waste that would be!

Lucky hated oppression with his whole heart. He used to call it a sin, but what he hated the most was people who are complacent, people who turn a blind eye to crime and corruption. He hated, with a passion, people who bribe and are bribed. Once when he was going on tour, I had just checked him and the band in at the airport and the lady who assisted us was so wonderful, I took out a R100 note and thanked her for her super service. He asked me what that was for and when I said for the good service, he was so angry with me! I couldn't understand what he was fussing about. He went for me there and then and told me that it was people like me who started this corrupt system. He said the woman would expect her next customer to do the same and if they didn't give her anything, she would stop the good service and behave as if she was doing people a favour when she was actually doing her job. He believed we get paid for what we do and don't deserve to be thanked in anything but words. "Rather take her details and buy her something or even encourage her by sending her flowers, if you feel you must," he said. He didn't say don't appreciate the good service, but there were ways of doing it and money was not one of them.

I learned from that day that I should carry little gifts with me, wherever I go, so that I can give one if I feel I want to. He believed that with each corruption there is a corruptor, and we often blame the receiving party even though they may not be the ones that started the corruption. We are the corruptors and we cry foul when the system turns against us.

I battled for a long time, and still do, to come to terms with the fact that this icon was murdered for a material possession – a mere motor car. Couldn't he have died for a better cause? Other heroes, like Steve Biko, were silenced for what they believed in, a worthwhile cause. The system thought they were silencing him but didn't realise that they were giving birth to busloads of Steve Bikos! He is stronger in his grave today than he would have been had he lived. However, having heard his stories, I doubt if he would have settled for half a loaf. If we still had Steve Biko, Chris Hani and the many great South Africans whose lives were destroyed before their time, we wouldn't have the cat fights that we see in the government today. Not to mention the deal of the day, which only serves a few intelligent people who have since been blinded by power and the dollar. You can, in fact, measure their intelligence – or lack of it – as they stoop lower and lower every day. I hope these intelligent

people of ours wake up from their sleep before it's too late. South Africans are losing patience.

Lucky had known deep in his heart that he would be taken out at some point in his life. If Steve Biko and Chris Hani died because of their beliefs, Lucky knew he didn't stand a chance. It didn't matter what car he was driving the day he was murdered, Lucky was going to die and he was going to die at the hands of criminals. The ironic part of it is that the people who killed Chris Hani were caught, and the people who killed Lucky Dube were also caught. With so many people getting away with murder, it makes you think. I sit and wonder if these arrests were erroneous, or if they were meant to happen. Just wondering. Are these arrests meant to prove that we have a security system that selects who it wants to arrest and who it would let get away with crime? I believe that Lucky had prepared for the day of his death. In fact, when that hour came, he knew it had come. We all have to die sometime, but most of us live on as if that day will never come. Lucky was one of the orderly ones.

2. HIS ESSENCE

I had always wondered what it was that attracted Lucky to the Shembe church, but as soon as I got to spend enough time with him, I got it. The message was loud and clear, the Shembe teachings made sense to the people who believed in themselves. Zulu people are proud of their culture; they've vowed to protect their legacy and teach other generations about the ways of their forefathers. Theirs is not a teaching that is taken from a passage in a book - their reference is based on real life issues, their daily issues and their rich history. They simply won't forget where they came from and are willing to preserve and protect their own history!

Their religion is still to date tending to their spiritual and ancestral gardens, planting the wisdom seed that many of its followers continue to connect with. This is one religion that understands that our traditions are not recognised as sources of substance regardless of the rich wisdom and good moral codes they represent.

I also agree that there is a spiritual truth that we must accept of our own before we can start believing in what others suggest who we should and should not be. Whether you are Jewish, Christian, Muslim etc, God is part of us all, this they teach their followers to understand that there is more to life than the daily rush.

What is worrying though is that inasmuch as Lucky understood the Shembe religion, there are thousands of people who believe Shembe to be their god, and they cannot be told otherwise. The prophet Shembe himself has taught them that he was a prophet sent to them by God and has explained the reasons he was sent. He has extolled the importance of being what God intended us to be, and never to think for one moment that we are inferior to any other nation. God's promises to us and his teachings make a lot of sense; it is vital that we're proud about being who we are and not losing ourselves to others and their beliefs.

Shembe teachings are about the Old and New Testaments and he teaches his people how to practice, maintain and pass on this wisdom from generation to generation, to them it is important to know that the past serves as a guide into the future, the young learn from the old. Someone asked me if they believed Jesus Christ was the son of God!

On our way to Rwanda for a show during the inauguration of their President in 2006, we opened the Bible to read an interesting chapter - Matthew 15:22-28. Lucky carried his Bible all the time, there were times when one would feel like telling this guy that look we are travelling, just leave me alone please, I need a break! Sometimes when you travel you need time with yourself, you just left your home and kids and need to deal with your stuff, lots of it, some exciting, some confusing and here is this person as if waiting for this moment to disturb your moment. At that time you had been working on this deal for no less than three months and now that you have gotten it together this is what happens, whooo... What do you do, this is Lucky Dube and you are at his service, no choice, no choice at all. Anyway, the verse reads: *22: And behold, a woman of Canaan came from that region and cried out to Him saying, "Have mercy on me, O Lord Son of David! My daughter is severely demon-possessed". 23: But he answered her not a word. And His disciples came and urged Him saying, "Send her away for she cries out after us". 24; But he answered and said, "I was not sent except to the lost sheep of the house of Israel". 25; Then she came and worshipped Him, saying "Lord help me". 26; But He answered and said, "It is not good to take the children's bread and throw it to the little dogs". 27; And she said, "Yes Lord, yet even the little dogs eat the crumbs which fall from their masters' table". 28; Then Jesus answered and said to her, "O woman, great is your faith! Let it be you as you desire" And her daughter was healed from that very hour.*

According to the Shembe teachings this scripture is taken literally, they believe that Jesus is the son of God who was sent to the Jews and not to everyone. I was almost offended by this misleading teaching of scripture, I thought. In fact I would like to believe that this is one of the most straightforward scripture about faith. If you read the whole chapter of Matthew 15, you get the full understanding of this gospel. This woman had so much faith in Jesus that nothing anyone did or said would turn her away from Him, she had her eyes fixed on Him. There was no indication that this woman felt insulted by what Jesus was saying, she wasn't discouraged by Jesus' words. He hadn't said "no" to her. He did say some stuff but this woman did not hear Him say "no". I have imagined Jesus, well yes I have, if He had said this to me and calling me this or that, I promise you He wouldn't have gotten away with it that easy! We always read about these sad stories in the newspapers and hear it in the news about women not knowing the meaning of a "no", when guys explain that women do say "no" but not actually meaning it? This is when a guy is in real trouble, and I mean real trouble. Women do say "no" and a "no" is a "no". It seems we understand this more than the guys do, Jesus had not said "no". And I think even if Jesus had said no this woman was not going to let go, she knew what she wanted from Jesus and nothing was going to get her to give up, not a no, not some harsh words, nothing.

I normally switch off from conversations of this sort when I feel like the Bible is being misinterpreted, I felt this way when Lucky was telling me this story. Jesus was not sent except to the lost sheep of Israel? What crap is this, Jesus was sent to all of us! I could not switch off, I had to put up an argument, a constructive informed argument at that but I have to make sure I understand where he is shooting from because Lucky Dube never raises things unless they are important. As I tried to tell him this scripture is about faith of our times, that the Shembe religion missed the very moral of the story, that Jesus was teaching us that if we seek Him although He was sent to the Jews He will be there for us. I was amazed at the boldness and honesty of Jesus' response to this woman, He didn't try to put it lightly, all that Jesus did was tell this woman the truth, bold, never tried to hide that He was sent to the Jews and in case this woman was not aware of it, He had to be honest and deliver the truth to her Himself. At the insistence of this woman Jesus showed her that even though He was sent to the lost nation of Israel that He will extend His compassion and help her. If you put yourself in the shoes of this woman like I have, such a statement would be offensive to say the least and I would like to believe that Jesus also said it the way He did with the sole intention of provoking this woman, testing to see if she really knows and understands who Christ is but instead she being the woman in need, she insisted that she also deserves to partake in the mercy of our Lord Jesus Christ. We are to learn from this story that in as much as this table was set for the Jews that we also can partake on it through Jesus our grace. If Jesus wasn't there an outsider this woman was, she wouldn't have qualified to eat off it. When we get deeper in conversation with Lucky, I often forget how grumpy I'd been when he started with his Bible this Bible that. I was raised in a church and did not discover the Bible now. I would always wonder why people get so excited to be talking about things that I've known from since I was a little girl. The Bible and God to me, not new, what's the fuss but nevertheless Lucky got me heated up every time we had a discussion, he knew me too well to know which buttons to press to get me started. Now I was at a point where I myself don't want to stop, the conversation was good, I felt good. He listened, he agreed with my understanding of this story. There was something he wanted to show me and my understanding of the scripture made it easier for him to continue. He started where I had left off, with this woman understanding who she was in Christ, an outsider. If indeed we understand who we are in Christ, why do we then follow religions which do not represent what Christ Himself represented. We argued with Lucky, a lot. I listened to him as he made his point, my mind was already made I was just listening because it was my turn to listen. The story of the woman of Canaan was a simple story period. What I didn't realize was that I spoke to the story in isolation, although I got the moral of it correct. I was also told the story in isolation, not taught the story and I stand risking to keep telling the story in isolation and whoever hears the story will believe because the story is genuine and has a moral lesson.

We cannot argue that Christ was sent to the lost nation of Israel, it is what it is, but what about us? What is God saying to us, are we also not lost? Is He implying that we should know where to go for our own problems? Why did God select a particular nation to bless and when they were lost He came to save them? What about us? These are the questions I ask, anyone coming across this scripture would also ask the same question, except those that are not taught the scriptures in isolation. Knowing who we are will assist us to go to Christ as we are, this is a critical point and each one of us can learn a lot from this story, if we listen to what God is telling us. Like I said if I was this woman Christ would have known me, where did He think this woman should go? He had been healing the sick and selectively so, I am sure when this woman went to Christ she knew she wasn't one of them, but so what? Lucky showed me the dangers of learning the scriptures in isolation and our approaches towards fearing telling Bible truths in case we are labelled. Christ did not expect this woman to be converted into a Jewish culture before He could assist her, He assisted her unconditionally. I still had my doubts because I was brought up as a Christian, I am grounded in what my Sunday school teacher taught me, what can Lucky teach me, he is an artist he cannot be teaching me about the Bible, I've been in this game long enough. I tried to put up resistance even though I could see his point, however, he said I understand where you're coming from rasta and you are not wrong, but this we must settle. By settling he means, now put on your thinking cap, we are about to start, when he does this always, I know we are going to argue until there is no room left for doubts. And we went on and on and on and on...

I finally realise that this word-battle is one I'm not going to win. I know the danger of scripture misinterpretation and how it can turn lives around, but I also know in my heart of hearts that some teachers of scripture just go over the Bible for fear of losing their followers and for this I am willing to listen to Lucky's point. It is easy for the interpretation of this scripture to provide a distraction of a good story whose intent has the potential to transform. God himself said it in *Hosea 4:6: "My people are destroyed for lack of knowledge. Because you have rejected knowledge. I also will reject you from being priest for Me. Because you have forgotten the law of your God. I also forget your children.* We read the Bible in church and don't read it at home by ourselves. We are so dependent on others to tell us God's truth, as if the Bible is limited to certain people for interpretation. If the truth is distorted we wouldn't even know, because we don't study our most important text book, the Bible.

There's nothing wrong with people following certain leaders of religion as long as they also partake in learning and trying to know God personally. People have a tendency to read the Bible only when and where they're told to read and this can turn disastrous, especially if they're easily brain-washed. They also choose a few relevant scriptures to back what they teach, and also choose which sets of rules apply to them and many of them are not found in the Bible. But Lucky's story was not only one sided. I've had to read the Bible over and over again to see if indeed what he was saying was what Jesus said. It was difficult having to leave my know it all attitude to start reading the Bible with an open mind, without influence from anyone. I've even had to buy my New King James Version at the Sheraton Hotel Lagos where we stayed on 30 December 2004 on our return from a show in Calabar Nigeria, I autographed it and wrote my first letter to God. That letter was written on January 17 of 2005, I share the letter, *Dear God, As I read your book please help me to understand what you want to show me today. As I learn more of you, please give me the desire to live the way you teach, I love you Lord. I find it difficult to know what to believe. Please help me to accept that even though I can't understand everything, I can always trust you and what you say in the Bible, I end it by saying, I love you Jesus.* Lucky pushed me to the limit, I've even had to buy a Bible in Nigeria! I couldn't wait to get home and read from my own Bible, I had to upgrade at that. The fear of God was instilled in me very early in my life and as you can see this letter to my God was nothing more than a plea to Him to help me be able to lift the right meaning out of whatever I might come across not to shake my standing with Him, I was sure after what Lucky showed me that I was going to find lots of stuff, I also suffered a disconnect not knowing if this is the right thing to do, or if I should continue with my life the way that it had been, this frustrated me a lot. At this point I was very afraid, but the reality of it all was that my approach to reading the Bible had changed and I was challenging the Man Himself, although I knew He knew this was going to happen I had to report my intentions and my new journey with Him. The scariest part was that the love of Jesus had set in my every fibre I wouldn't know how to live without Him, just like a child who is brought up knowing that a certain parent is their parent only to find out later in life that it wasn't so. This caused me to suffer some disconnect which left me drained for days. There had been a lot of good things that had happened in my life which only the hand of God could have been responsible for, I felt Him too. I pleaded to God to take responsibility for what I was about to go through, my new journey. I promised myself that my approach would be as critical and honestly as I could, I will go one second, one minute, one hour, one step at a time and review the Bible. I realized that if I chose not to know God on my own, then I would have no one to blame if what I had been taught all along was wrong. I've also asked God to guide me through this review as I search deeper to find out the truth. I call it review because I already knew some of the scriptures and have heard many sermons, so this would be a review for me. We have many Bibles at my house each of my children accounts to more than one my mother had them in different languages, colours and sizes too, so when I bought this Bible in Lagos I had heard that its interpretations are better than most Bibles. I spoilt myself and had to keep a constant reminder for myself so that if I come across some conflicting stuff, I would have already pleaded my case with God, I may not understand everything but that which I don't understand let me not put my own meaning to, let me understand exactly the way it is supposed to be understood. So if my Bible tells me that Jesus did say to the Woman of Canaan He was sent to the lost nation of Israel and all the other things He said, I will not put meaning to a straight forward text, and this time, my time of reviewing I will not put my own meaning to this scripture other than what it really says. Difficult as it was for me to start embracing this journey, I approached it with sincerity and at the same time I also felt betrayed, having thought I was raised well, raised as a Christian. I've had to deal with me and my new approach to the holy book knowing that there are serious problems with what I was raised to believe, I always thought that that was it, end of story, and this time I also felt that if this is true then what?

We have to understand that it's difficult for us humans to know and understand everything God tells us in the Bible. For that reason there are those whom we will need guidance from, those that have the gift of discernment, those who will be given the gift of interpreting God's word and those who will teach it and those who will listen and understand. Not everyone can interpret the Bible, and God's spirit is needed to understand it. But that also presents challenges in churches in that, God speaks to people from the same church, (one with a gift to interpret and the other who can teach), He gives each a message but conflicting messages, you know what I mean, the God said messages we often hear at church! Most of the time the messages would be about the vision of the church for that year, say the one leader is given a message to plant another church in the Eastern part of the city, and the other says God said the Western part. How would we come to the conclusion which is God's real message? They both are good leaders in the same church and have been for a very long time, how do we distinguish between the two which is God's will for that church? The very leaders have no doubt that God spoke to them and He has spoken to them before but this time this particular message is conflicted, my point is, we often pray that God will show us His will for the church, but when faced with such challenges, instead of staying strong together and relying on God to further guide us in our faith, we divide the church of God. I am raising this point to accept the fact that the Bible is conflicted, we are bound to be conflicted too for we are human, we should not run away from this truth for we are then making God a liar by avoiding Bible truths. God did not write the Bible, humans did, and they did their best, protecting human errors can only lead us to disastrous conclusions. My second journey with the Bible began then, when there was something difficult or something puzzling, I would go back to Lucky and ask if he would help with his wisdom. Today I ask the same question was Christ was sent to the lost nation of Israel?

Searching my heart to answer this vexing question, I've opened the Bible many and I mean many times on my own to find out if Jesus was actually sent only to God's favoured nation, the Jews. It is clear that this is true. And again I would like to believe that this was so the scriptures could be fulfilled! In this new journey of the Bible I no longer read to understand, I read so I can over-stand, I absorb and perceive so I can discern to make sure I do not stand under God's word. Those that read the Bible would understand that God promised His chosen nation that He would send them a prophet like them in *Deuteronomy 18:18, "I will raise up for them a Prophet like you from among their brethren, and will put My words in His mouth, and He shall speak to them all that I command Him"* I've always known that the prophet referred to in Deuteronomy was Jesus Christ, and it is so because my Sunday school teacher said so! Well it helped to go to Sunday school, this is where I was taught whenever you see a capital He, Him, His, Me, My, Prophet in the middle of a Biblical text, you know that this refers to God or Jesus. And in the New Testament, well, my New King James special Bible has Jesus' words in red, whenever I come across red text, I know Jesus is speaking! And my point inasmuch as God raises up different prophets at different times, the Prophet He made mention of in Deuteronomy was in reference to the promise He made to the children of Israel, that Prophet was Jesus, God had long promised his chosen nation that He will send them a Prophet to save them, if you further read verse 19 of Deuteronomy, God makes it clear that there would be other prophets and He is referring to them in small letter "p". Now my case with Mr Dube is settled, this story was worth listening to, worth defending and yes it broadened my horizon. I share the story of the woman of Canaan with pride, privilege and a duty. The pride that Lucky opened a new world for me, the courage to approach the Bible truthfully without fear, without influence from anyone and look at the Bible from different angles trusting that God will show me what He wants me to see and understand. I am no longer afraid to engage God on what I think is conflicting stuff in the Bible, I can go to Him boldly, I have my own view of the Bible and I am able to review the stories in the Bible, the sea of confusion is gone with the wind. The privilege not so many people will get in their lifetime, to be a part of a humbling story like Lucky's. The many stories he shared with me have become my treasure, some very personal, so personal I will have to take them to my grave. The privilege to see multitudes lined in streets just to honour him, old and young, rich and poor, they all came in their numbers. The privilege of walking the red carpets, the privilege to be my brother's keeper, when he is quiet, I can still shout on his behalf. The duty to share an African story so noble, the duty to continue his legacy to walk a mile in his shoes for this is a duty that makes my heart beat. Let me steal wise words from the Ultimate Warrior, James Brian Hellwig, an American professional wrestler, a day before he passed on, *"Every man's heart one day beats its final beat, his lungs breath their final breath. And if what that man did in his life, makes the blood pulse through the body of others, and makes them believe deeper in something larger than life, then his essence, his spirit will be immortalized by the storytellers, by the loyalty, by the memory of those who honour him and make whatever the man did live forever"*. Need I say more, thank you for the words of wisdom the Ultimate Warrior may your soul rest in peace. I treasure my Bible so much these days, I look at it and I know I want to open it and find out what God is saying, that the world has missed many times before. Lucky tried to teach through his music, I have listened to the music more and more and the more

34

I listen to it the more it continues to broaden my knowledge outside the narrow circle of the religion that was presented to my ancestors to replace my culture. And now that he is gone I've discovered amazing stuff like the teachings of the Bible are similar to moral codes found in culture, and he is no longer here to share this with. There is one thing that amazes me too, that when it comes to matters of morality it seems that all religions are in agreement with God, all cultures agree with God on morality but we continue to disagree with one another on trivial things. The discrepancies found in the Bible, the God said messages, the unclear texts, the legitimacy that we all seem to want to be right about, the abuse of Bible teachings for personal gains, all of these are the cause of our problems today, these are the reasons we have so much hatred for one another. We are however happy to continue our journeys without attempting any solution except to claim that we are right and others are wrong. I am in no way suggesting that nations should be rigid with their cultures in these ever changing times, we can learn to adjust behaviors to be in sync with these changing times, but there are certain things that we need not compromise on our cultures. Whatever Jesus' mission was, it was clear, He Himself made it clear. He helped this woman unconditionally and she was not required to practice what the chosen nation practiced. The tradition of Jewish people as God's chosen nation was different to her own, she came to Jesus for healing, got it and I am sure she went and served God in her own tradition.

I realise that the same culture I'm being discouraged against is the connection I need to connect with to prepare me to connect with my Lord. For in my culture you will find respect, love, peace and unity which the religion that was forced to me came and scattered into many confusing pieces. James said faith without works is dead, Paul said salvation comes through faith, they said these things because God told them to say that, I cannot sit here and point fingers at the different ways they presented the gospels, what I am aware of is they were human, I will not turn what they said around and put my interpretations to them. It is important to note that, it was the Jews who needed saving because they were given the law, none of us were given the law. God needed to redeem them for they are that important for Him, Him and they had a binding contract, they are His chosen nation, I am not. I am not part of that history, but I continue to learn from their history. I am a strong black woman, I owe my roots and values to the Bakgatla Ba Mmakau, to these roots I owe everything. God loves me where I am, I am His child just here where I am. However, God has also allowed me to borrow knowledge from the historical stories of His people, learning from the teachings and obeying all that he commanded. And all that He commanded is already present in my culture in the tribe of Bakgatla ba Mmakau. In that community I learned to love God, my neighbour and myself, I learnt patience with God, my neighbour and self, I learnt peace with God, my neighbour and self, I learnt kindness with God, my neighbour and self, I learnt forgiveness with God (yes forgiveness with God, and I have forgiven God too), my neighbour and self and I have had joy with God, my neighbour and self. All of these teachings that Christ taught in parables to His own, I have learnt from my own, not in parables but in practice, in real life, in real time. In a very poor community, with no Godly promises, but life had to go on, we are not children of the promise and we understand this does not make us less than human.

The music of Lucky Dube tried in its splendour to unite the scattered pieces of our cultural rhythms, to weave back the pieces of our cultures' cirles, to give us purpose and meaning that we lost through this confusion presented to us in the name of God says and the Bible says. Lucky never said to me do not believe in Jesus Christ. Not once. He got me to think deep, to be independent of what was sown into me so I could be free to find my own purpose and meaning of life, he freed me from many years of mental slavery.

The question I was asked, do you believe if the Shembe religion believes Christ is the son of God, is a very shallow question, it sounds stupid sometimes. Is Christ the son of God? What does the Bible say about this, it is documented aint it? If you are your

36

mothers' child do I have to believe that you are when you say so? Even if I wasn't there to prove that you are indeed what you tell me. Is it nine O'clock now? Is it your nine O'clock now? It may be nine O'clock for a Chinese person in South Africa now, but it is not necessarily nine O'clock for a Chinese person in China right now. What is this believing we often argue about, that the history of Jewish people is what it is?. And we can fight over it, forcing our ways through that which is written and confirmed? Certain things we subject each other to are sometimes baffling.

Instead of teaching that which Christ commanded us, and admitting to those that follow us that the Bible was written by people like us and it is the way it is, we prefer not. I've asked myself this many times, only God can defend the Bible not humans. Humans will use the Bible to their own advantages and for some reason they know they can get away with it for they know we don't read it ourselves.

Yes Christ is the son of God, do I believe? Yes I do believe. I believe the stories of the Bible. I believe I can live a full life, with commitment and conviction, with respect for everything and everyone. As I journey through life, I'll take my culture with and nothing changes my belief in God, I will go to Him as a strong black woman, not suffering from an identity crisis, I belong to God as I am, I'll go to my mother's grave when I feel like it and will not be ashamed of it for it is not pagan, it's my culture. I will take all my beliefs with, the belief that I am an equal partner in God's kingdom, I will slaughter if I have to, this is my culture, I'll go to God with all I have, my weakness, my strengths, I will take all to Him, without any stigma, I am not prejudiced, I do not feel any shame about my culture, I am aware of the depth of my culture and history, this is where God wants me, not there! Jesus Himself said whoever believes in the Father also believe in Him.

I will not try and assimilate to a culture I do not identify with, a culture that comes dressed in a beautiful Bible form and justifies its own barbaric manipulation of others using the Bible. To me what matters is my sincere commitment to humanity. I stumbled on a quote by an Indian philosopher and spiritual visionary, Sri Aurobindo on the benefits of religion from different groups, he says:

"Each religion has helped mankind.

1.Paganism increased in man the light of beauty, the largeness and height of his life, his aim at a many sided perfection

2. Christianity gave him some vision of divine love and charity

3. Buddhism has shown him a noble way to be wiser, gentler, purer

4. Judaism and Islam how to be religiously faithful in action and zealously devoted to God

5. Hinduism has opened to him the larges and profoundest spiritual possibilities.

A great thing would be done if these God-visions could embrace and cast themselves into each other, but intellectual dogma and cult-egoism stand in the way."

Wow, what a beautiful quote from a wise man, may your soul rest in perfect peace great one!

My exodus, finds resonance in Sri Aurobindo's profound statement, "Each religion has helped mankind" *A great thing would be done if these God-visions could embrace and cast themselves into each other, but intellectual dogma and cult-egoism stand in the way."*

I've drawn strength from this profound statement, and I've had to admit that it seems it is hard for the Shembe religion to embrace Christianity for various reasons, one of which is very critical. To them Christianity appears to be an open-for-abuse type of system. It is my opinion that they would rather protect their own moral value system, one that they feel has not been upheld in the Christian

38

church. The modern church does not represent what they believe to be the core foundation of humanity. I am also in support and share the same view when it comes to their moral value system. They refuse to use the cross as an excuse for man to do as they will. When we Christians are found in situations we cannot explain we always refer to the cross and use pre-package unrelated scriptures to back our actions. To them moral values cannot be bent, they cannot be replaced.

It would be interesting if we all tried to cast ourselves into each other, because clearly it seems we all are striving to help mankind, the problem is our cult - egoism and the dogmas stand in our ways, we make others look bad and refer to them as cults. I sit and wonder how we can possibly measure each others' meanings and purposes against our own faiths. The word cult creates a great amount of confusion for many religious and non-religious people. I went through the internet to search and learn what cults are, I have come to one conclusion which is that if I continued with my search I would end up referring to every religion, every group as cults, I will not quote any examples either! My point exactly is that if a group is worshipping God differently they are considered an unhealthy or destructive group from a Christian perspective. Everyone calls everyone a cult with many groups contending they are the only true Church, and that all Christians outside that particular group are following a deficient Gospel and a false Christ. With so many denominations and religions, how can one know which one is real when they themselves criticize one another as if there is some sort of competition when it comes to serving God. Christianity just like other groups do slip into cult-like behaviors from time to time, this due to the fact that they each adopt unique ways that define the way they worship and when they remain steadfast in such behaviors these become cult like. Lucky followed a religion that encouraged him to nurture his spirit of discernment and connect with his original source.

In my journey of trying to over-stand the things of God I discovered we all need a chance in life, a chance to make our own choices,

choices which are not influenced by politics and religion. I also realize you cannot make an informed decision of your choice if you do not know who you are and that's a fact. I find a lot of truth in this profound statement *"A great thing would be done if these God-visions could embrace and cast themselves into each other, but intellectual dogma and cult-egoism stand in the way."*

Perhaps this will enable others to embrace Christ from where they are, and yes embrace Christ with truth. The Christians will also embrace their respective cultures and accept others from where they are.

I have learned to take everything to Jah, as Lucky would put it, Take it to Jah.

All this pain in this world

All the crying in this world

I'll take it to Jah

All the worries in this world

And all the troubles in this world

I will take it to Jah

Lucky's understanding of God was that He Himself said no one will be turned away if he believes, he says no one will be rejected, because I am your father. He said even when satan comes with demons, turn everything I believed in upside down, I will never forget, with Jah on our side, who can be against us.

I had a conversation with a friend the other day about the things of God and how unaware we are that God shows up in our lives all the time. For her, God showed up in her kitchen through *Matthew 6:33. "But seek first the kingdom of God and his righteousness, and all these things will be added to you"*. She told me that she'd heard the words many times before, but suddenly, she felt the reference directed to her as a person. She was alone in her kitchen and the scripture just hit her right between the eyes and she got it! Her eyes were opened, her ears heard it and the message was loud and clear.

"I didn't need an interpreter, it was as if the words had been spoken out loud – to me alone," she said in elation. "But it was also clear that there was a condition in this scripture, a demanding condition." I raised my eyebrows in question and asked, "What is the demand? And she answered - To seek God's kingdom first as the core thing, not the other way round like in the modern day, we do other things and we later demand that God should clean up after we've messed up."

My friend's discovery was a great testimony for me. I had known her a little over six years and hearing this from her was the greatest thing that could have happened to me there and then. It confirmed that the gospel of Jesus Christ has been given to people in isolation. The core of our lives is the love of God, his righteousness, grace and mercy. Those who are in Christ, who have sought the kingdom of God and his righteousness need not be reminded to do good. It was ironic also that Lucky gave a lesson of the woman of Canaan in Matthew, my friend also referred to her moment with God referring to Matthews account. As if they both were saying these gospels are for us to learn from.

But what exactly does it mean to seek first the kingdom of God and His righteousness? What do we need to do? Does this mean joining a particular church, becoming a committed member, following all the rules of that church?

Seeking first the kingdom of God is a personal thing between man and God. Going to church is secondary; we go to church for fellowship. But a true relationship with God makes it easy for us to fit in at the right church and it's easy to serve Him with understanding. Our personal understanding of God becomes the centre of all who believe in Him. The church is a common ground for all believers. But first have a personal relationship with God, what you learn at church should be good news that motivates you throughout your journey of faith. You won't be confused by what you should or shouldn't believe. Thank you, Nikiwe.

Lucky's journey in his faith saw him compose a song about the religion he followed. The song, titled "Shembe is the way" highlights the importance of upholding one's culture and tradition. It is through this culture that we learn who we truly are. He wrote about how other religions undermine the black culture and make others feel inferior. He had been trying to join a church but the more he went to other churches the more confused he became. It wasn't easy for him to find a spiritual home, one that could simplify the most complex spiritual challenges that he faced. When he discovered the Shembe church he was almost at the point of giving up on religion. Nothing made sense, the teachings undermined what he believed in and as a result of that he referred to that moment as 'walking in the valley of death.'

He could not hide his excitement at acknowledging that he was lost at some point in his life. When he realised it he sought to learn the truth from this culture, from the wise men who preserved what was important from the beginning as *Proverbs 1:5 puts it "wise man will hear, and will increase learning ; and a man of understanding shall attain unto wise counsel"* Lucky discovered his wise counsel, he heard and increased his learning. I've been to many churches I find Christians who are able to quote scripture like you cannot believe it, I've not seen or heard wisdom from these Christians, others even criticizing their own cultures. What are we saying to the generations that will come after us, that it is okay to live freely as we wish as long as we are saved? That all they need to do is work so they can make money and live comfortably, as if that is what life requires for us to be. We are practicing a culture that as long as you believe Christ as your Lord and Saviour that all is well, a culture influenced by our inconsistencies, confusions and frustrations caused by our inability to stand right with God. We leave our children and their children's children a legacy of our shaken cultures which was offered as a replacement but is causing us suffering, it enslaves us mentally. This is what we are leaving for our children, we inherited this from our elders, we seem to be trapped in this system and we seem not to have a way out, this is what Lucky Dube was advocating. There is a way out and this way out comes through knowing who we are, what we are and where we are going. Lucky was trying to enlighten me, what he was doing was to ensure that my position in the Lord is the way it should be, without influence from outside. I listen to Shembe is the way differently, I do not interpret the song, I just enjoy the way he sends the message to his fans. We all have our Shembe's, throughout the whole world, that God send to us to listen to, it is up to us to choose if we are willing to listen to them or follow systems that enslave us. Who would I be if I didn't know anything about where I come from, but I know the origin of others who are not an inch related to me, I know their story better than I know mine, pray in their language better than I can pray in my own, who would I be.

The comments made on the internet after his death stirred a lot of emotions within me. I was at some point tempted to correct the misunderstanding, but I thought sometimes you need to let people say what they have to say and when the time is right for correction then you do it without letting yourself get emotional. Some people were concerned that Lucky was following a cult. The comments were nothing but offensive to me personally, because I knew what Lucky believed in. We have a tendency as people to listen to what we want to hear, read what we want and processing of information is distorted in our minds. I don't understand why some people have the tendency to speak for us about us and it is people who do not even know who they are themselves. If Lucky wanted to say Shembe was the way to heaven he would have said it as explicitly as it should be. He was never afraid to say things the way they should be said.

This is a song that is straightforward, about respecting fellow human beings and what they believe in traditionally. The song goes like this:

It was in the valley of death, I was walking in

It was the valley of confusion for many years

Different religions, different beliefs

Looking down upon my tradition

Making fun of my language

Telling my children, they have no God

Finally I can tell them about

Shembe is the way

Lucky was serving God, not Shembe. Shembe was the way to guide his followers to the culture, beliefs and practices observed by Zulu people, protocols which were passed down from their great-grandparents.

Oh Shembe thank you for showing us the way

Shembe nobunazaretha

Oh Shembe thank you for healing my people

Shembe nobunazaretha

Shembe is the way

No one will undermine my religion

No one will undermine my culture anymore

Cause God sent him from above, to be with the people

Bring them back to what is their own

Take them back to the ways of our forefathers

Finally I can tell generation and generations

That Shembe is the way

Chorus

Oh Shembe THANK YOU FOR SHOWING US THE WAY

Shembe Nobunazaretha

If you read the above without interpreting it or trying to find what the song doesn't say, it should be straightforward as it is. But if you are going to interpret the song and want to add your own meaning then you might find yourself with the same problem the Bible is facing. He loved God with all of his heart but the way the gospels were being taught didn't make sense to him, and when he discovered the teachings of Shembe he knew this was the way he preferred to serve his God.

The Shembe religion regularly observes certain traditions found in the Old Testament. These included observing the Sabbath, certain prayers, and converging on the holy mountain. "The followers of the Shembe religion are called Nazarites; they don't undermine other religions like Christianity, Judaism, Hinduism, Islam or traditional religions. They wouldn't abandon their culture and traditions for anything. They believe every man should serve God from where he is without intruding and undermining others' cultures, and competing about who is right and who is not. They are of the belief that their church is as good to them as yours is good to you. God is in all of us.

I personally battled to understand the Shembe religion in the beginning. I think this was due to the fact that the first Shembe was apparently a prophet. I do believe that he was God-chosen, sent to

45

lead the people who were to follow him. I have difficulty also understanding that if the first leader was sent by God, why then is there a succession issue within this religion? Why is the religion kept within the family as if it was some kingdom system with a throne and heirs to the throne?

The ongoing fighting within the church regarding who should lead and who should be next in line has been worrying to me. And like so many other churches today, it seems churches belong to families. It seems to me that God's work has suddenly become more of a business where people fight amongst themselves. I'm not sure what they fight about - whether it is the leadership or the church funds. I've always understood that people have differences everywhere, even in the church, but this is the first time I've encountered a situation where courts are involved in God's work. This being the case, I wonder if it isn't a danger to the followers of certain leaders.... I wonder which leader I would choose if I were in the middle of all this, or rather, which leader would have wanted me to follow him .... this is just me wondering, I hope you understand. To me, the church epitomises the centre of harmony, peace and love, not conflict.

It worries me that this friction might even lead to the loss of lives, thank God so far I haven't heard of any incidents.. And of course in this day and age man is free to choose that which makes sense to him, but at the same time I do understand why the Shembe teaching is what it is, their culture. They understand the importance of doing good versus choosing that which feels good on the surface. They know that culture represents responsibility and respect,

I am also of the view that blessings and certain Godly gifts are not transferable - or maybe I'm mistaken? People can follow certain teachings and be able to teach others but I'm not sure how gifts such as prophecy can be transferred from a father to a son etc. Are these gifts not supposed to come from God Himself, blessing those that He wants to bless and give gifts to? Just wondering as I learn more about the culture... Should I rather say that those who came after

46

the first Shembe are the teachers of the religion? My understanding
of prophets is that they are chosen and raised by God they are
moulded and trained by Him. I also have to admit my understanding
of a prophet was limited to what I was taught in our church. The
only prophets that we ever heard of were Biblical and as a result we
grew up believing a prophet is someone who has the gift of
prophesy and could tell the future, we had none in our church. It is
for that reason that people will always sneak out of their churches to
go seek a prophet's help elsewhere. The Bible teaches us about
different prophets and from this I have learnt that some of the
people God appointed to carry His work were also referred to as
prophets. Anyone who carried a message for God is referred to as a
prophet. Some were priest who had the gift of prophesy but others
were just prophets and not necessarily priests. Most teachers of the
scriptures would tell us at some point or another that "God said",
they would have encounters with God and they carry God's
messages all the time, I would like to think that these people are
also prophets. So back to my church, does this mean that God did
not appoint any prophets for us or is it because the religion that was
forced to us decided there was no need for us to know and
acknowledge our own prophets? I am asking the God that I know
now, if He had no message for us even when He saw our sufferings
then? Maybe I am just being ahead of myself, maybe it was true
God did not see a need to send us our own prophets because what
that church stood for then was not what He had ordained. Or maybe
those that forced religion to us decided to hide the truth about
prophets just in case God revealed Himself to us and His will for us.

Lucky and I had countless discussions on culture and the Bible. I
was of the view that culture complicates my life, while he was
cultural. Having been raised in a Christian family, I'm grounded in
the teachings of both the Old and New Testaments. I guess, I, like
many of my fellow brothers and sisters, am an offspring of a lost
culture, following a religion that was forced on my ancestors. I'm
not in any way related to Dutch people, but for some odd - and I
mean peculiar reason! I was raised in a Dutch- influenced church

called "Nederduitse Gereformeerde Kerk in Afrika" (NG), a Dutch reformed church. To date I cannot explain what influenced my parents to follow this religion, one thing that I know is that they loved God.

If it hadn't been for the brave men and women of our times, I would still be stuck with this religion, not knowing how to use my right and apply the scriptures in my life. When religion was introduced to my ancestors, they believed everything they were told, not knowing that they were being manipulated and robbed of their birthrights, their riches and the future of many generations to come. My future - I am in this mess today because of that!

I went to a memorial service of a friend's mother the other day, may your sweet soul rest in God's eternal peace Mrs Theresa Ephenia Senne from a township near my village in Mmakau. The women there were fired up on the Lazarus scripture. I had heard the scripture so many times before that I would also be able to preach that sermon! This scripture is normally preached as a scripture of faith in Christ. Lazarus had been buried a few days and his body was at a decomposing stage, this scripture teaches that if we believe in Christ nothing is impossible. What I didn't bargain for that day was to experience something beyond what had become a tradition of the Bible. My people have gotten it, they preached on the Lazarus sermon from different angles, something I was not expecting, The one woman stood up and did her thing, came from a totally different angle, she said notice Jesus does not go to Lazarus in the tomb, she said instead Jesus calls Lazarus by his name and says to him step up Lazarus, come to me. For me this was like wow, our people are getting it, gone are the days when church pre-packaged teachings is what we hear day in and day out, we are also stepping up, saying the things that God is telling us to say, to not only rely on the ministers of religion to preach to us. I learnt from this scripture that God also calls us unto Himself, and we need to come just as we are. Not only did this woman reveal our need to heed to God's calling, but also that we can go to Him and tell Him a piece of our mind. As Jesus came back from His mission, Mary the sister of Lazarus gave it to

48

Jesus, saying if You were here on time, my brother would not have
died, she blamed Jesus for her brother's death as if her brother
should have lived forever. We are quick to blame God if He doesn't
answer our prayers when we want Him to. We do not like to abide
by God's timing, we are quick to give up when we suspect we have
done everything we could and nothing is working out forgetting
God works on His will and timing for our lives not ours.. But you
need to take your position, Lazarus' sister took her position, she told
Jesus, Your friend. Who are we in Christ? How do we approach
Him, with fear and humbleness that we were raised to? When you
have a right to something, sometimes you call it what you ought to
call it, treat it with whatever emotion. At this Jesus did not only call
Lazarus back to life, He gave Lazarus a chance to make a choice, to
not look at his rotting condition, to step up in his condition and get
his healing. If only our religious confines could give us a chance to
make these choices in our lives to come to Jesus as we are, we have
some traditional businesses that needs to be attended to, but we are
so afraid of what the church will say. We are afraid because we
have heard the church has its own commandments, at this we cannot
heed Jesus' invitation to come out of our tombs, we remain
spiritually blind because we fear the church commandments which
at times are not Biblical. In my culture if someone dies in an
accident or is murdered, traditionally there is a ritual that needs to
be performed to ensure the spirit of that person doesn't hover
around. Church says its pagan to perform that ritual, culture says if
you do not do it, it will cause problems for the family and hurt
innocent people. This ritual is performed in different forms, some
would use a tree branch, whereas others use snuff, whatever form
one uses to connect spiritually. Elders will then lead the ritual and
guide the spirit of the dearly departed after which it is re-connected
to the body and then buried. This if not done, causes problems. It
doesn't have to make sense to others but the point is that we need to
respect cultures even if we do not understand and accept that in life
we cannot understand everything. And just because you do not
understand it does not mean it does not exist. Your tradition is as
good to you as mine is good to me. If we stopped to criticise and

ridiculed one another's cultures we can collectively find peace and freedom, justice and compassion, harmony and love that we so desperately seek. What we all need is the spiritual solidarity to understand that we are together as one, God is part of us all. Lucky sang about it hear it in your heart.

One of the things that baffle me also is the concern that others have about if the Roman Catholics would go to Heaven. Apparently because of their religious approach of honouring Maria, the mother of Jesus. I often wonder if we really apply our minds when we criticise one another, when we claim to know who will go to Heaven and who won't. The same question could be asked about us, Just what if God wanted us to be who we were in the first place. How can Jews cease to be Jews? What happens to their birth rights?

Lucky and I would often argue to a point where my own faith would be in question. He would always reference his point to show that he understood what he was talking about.

I still maintain that scriptures shouldn't be interpreted in a way that feels right for a certain group only. I am now playing devil's advocate; the house of Shembe is guarding their legacy, a legacy that might be diluted and neutralised should they let outsiders run with it.

A brief historical overview tells us that Isaiah Mdliwamafa Shembe was born near the Drakensberg some time round about 1870. His mother, Sitheya, was a lovely young girl who had been chosen by God to be the mother of the Prophet. Once when walking alone in the mountains, she heard a voice saying, "My daughter, don't pollute yourself with beer-drinking and becoming involved with men. You will one day give birth to the Servant of God." She was stunned and didn't understand where the voice came from.

On another occasion, she and a group of young girls had been working in the wheatfields, tying up their own bundles. When they left to go and eat their meal a strong wind came up and destroyed all of the bundles, except those of Sitheya. The girls all fell back in amazement, telling her that she was protected.

Another time, when the girls were all together collecting firewood, they found a flower of unsurpassed beauty in the forest. Sitheya picked it and put it in her mouth, and the Holy Spirit went into her womb. Her husband-to-be had already been chosen by God. His name was Mayekisa and when he and his family had paid the dowry of cattle, the marriage ceremonies were strictly observed according to Zulu custom.

When Sitheya fell pregnant, the Holy Spirit moved out and another child, not Shembe, was born. There were a few children born before Shembe but they all passed away, because it was ordained that he would be the eldest son.

When she was six months pregnant with Shembe, Sitheya began to see white-clad people in her dreams and again heard a voice reminding her that she would give birth to the Servant of God. And when he was born, quickly and without complications, she was happy and realised that everything she'd been told had come true.

His father named his son Mdliwamafa-ezwe but his grandfather called him Shembe, and that was his name from then on; it also became the family name.

He was the founder of the church known as the Nazarite church and led it from 1910 till 1935. He was succeeded by His Holiness Johannes Galilee Shembe from 1935 till 1976. After his death the church divided into two factions and in 2009, it divided again into four factions, three in KwaZulu-Natal and one in Gauteng.

I am of the view that if there was no Shembe to bring God's people back to what is their own and take them back to the ways of our fathers, who would? Religion was never meant to replace culture. The two can co-exist, but there are times when I feel my culture is undermined. A people's culture cannot be replaced by religion, which was designed to replace culture when it was used as a weapon by the oppressors. The Shembe religion seems to understand that and people are taught who they really are, where they come from and the lessons they need to learn from religion.

I believe that there were other cultures before nations were introduced to religion, that there was understanding among these nations. That's why nations have their own cultures, some nations have guarded their own cultures since, they've made sure it remained intact and no foreign influences were allowed, I guess we also need to go one step back and weave together that which the evil system destroyed and stole. Culture is culture and religion is religion - period. I have seen the Shembe people in action, in their praising moods doing their cultural thing whilst at the same time worshipping and praising God the best way they know how. They have done this from time immemorial; why would they now be expected to change their culture and adopt something that was presented to them as a replacement? They have embraced the Bible; they read it in their language and apply it the way it is written.

Without the true understanding of your own culture it becomes easy to lose sight of who you are. Our cultures' seasons and circles have never moved in the same rhythms as the religion that was being forced on our forefathers. Back when the oppressors' intention was to separate the family unit by keeping the head away from the family for long periods, they knew that if your true source of life had been disconnected you couldn't remain intact. You will believe in anything and everything, thinking that the system will bring you better things. Culture is everything.

Lucky Dube strived in his spiritual path to learn and truly feel that there's always access to us staying connected to our true rhythms and circles without following religions and teachings our forefathers never identified with. Why didn't Lucky live one more year, do one more track, just one more album, do one more tour, just maybe do one more newsletter, maybe just one more prayer....?

This is the part of the story where I'm reminded of Bob Marley's song "Exodus." – Movement of God's people.. Bob Marley expresses the importance of true leadership, a leadership of purpose and promise. He reminds us not to forget who we are, where we come from and where we're going. He borrows from the stories of the Jews (the Bible) that we also need to return to the ways of our fathers, return to what is ours eventually. We need another Moses to get us attuned to our cultural circles and rhythms; what we don't need is a system that enslaves us mentally. Anything and everything seems right to us because we were told our cultures weren't good enough for us and therefore were replaced by other systems. Although we loved God our understanding of Him was so twisted, we missed our true connection with Him.

The one thing that will haunt me for the rest of my life is Lucky's approach to African shows. He believed that if he didn't have a message to deliver to Africa, he wouldn't do a show. I am talking about a region with the highest demand in relation to the rest of the world, but he would refuse to go back because of popular demand. Doing work in Africa was never about the money he made; it's clear that this was about the work he was doing in Africa, delivering the "message" of love and unity. It still doesn't make sense to me why he didn't create a message every year so some of us could just go and make an extra dollar! He was concerned by whether the messages were heard by the people more than how much money he made out of the shows. How good would the messages be if they cannot inspire, sink in and be over-stood. You can make as many albums and money as you can but if the message is going nowhere how is this going to fulfill your purpose and meaning in life? This was Lucky's very essence, admirable.

Again, if he were still alive we would have something to argue about, it is like the only way he could get me to over-stand him was if he starts an argument with me. From a spiritual point of view he knew in his heart that he was a messenger to the parts of the world where his message was relative; he was not driven by greed or popularity.

Today I sit and wonder and want to ask another question. Did Africa hear Lucky? Did we even listen to the cultural rhythm of the music? Do we love his music just because it was popular or are we going to get it at some point or another? What was the message, I've asked myself several times. How many have heard this message, what are we going to do with the message? I've followed every single comment made after Lucky was murdered. These comments all have one thing in common, yes it will be hard to break through the hard shells of the system but if we strive to take one step back and look into who we are we will be able to start bringing change within our respective faiths and cultures, we will learn to be critical thoughtful weavers of our own cultures. This as we strive to learn to respect and tolerate one another will lead to a path where we are all guided by a true source within the soul of each one of us. Stay strong, for God has heard your cry, Africa. God feels your pain, hold on, press on and take all your worries to Him. Guard against other values intruding into the African culture, it is ours, let's protect it. Jah will guide and protect you, my Africa.

One of the strongest points he ever made in my life was when he challenged me on whether I believed God would punish Jews for not believing Jesus Christ was their promised Messiah. He would say even though Jesus Christ was sent to them, they didn't believe what the Bible confirmed through the story of the woman of Canaan in the gospel according to *Matthew 15:22-28*. He would ask me: do you think God will reverse the promise He made to the Jews? God said they will remain His favoured nation forever.

Lucky and I would debate endlessly, but his arguments were always supported by scripture. The whole chapter of Romans 9 which is about God's sovereign choice explains it even better:

"These are my kinsmen according to the flesh. They are Israelites, and to them belongs the adoption, the glory, the covenants, the giving of the law, the worship and the promises. To them belong the patriarchs, and from their race, according to the flesh, is the Christ who is God over all, blessed forever. Amen. But it is not as though

the word of God has failed. For not all who are descended from Israel belong to Israel, and not all are children of Abraham because they are his offspring, but through Isaac shall your offspring be named. This means that it is not the children of the flesh who are the children of God, but the children of the promise are counted as offspring".

He had a very unique way of looking at the gospels; he simply said, "you see Rasta, this was to fulfill the scriptures. The story of Jacob and Esau in the Bible is a perfect example and proof of this fact. Poor Esau was Isaac's offspring and by his birthright he deserved to be blessed by his father, but unfortunately the blessing ended with Jacob and it was approved by God Himself."

He would say that just because someone was influenced by the church and had heard the word, they were children of the promise. You can be a part of the visible church but not the invisible church. Lucky was well read, reading about other religions including Judaism and Islam. According to what God had promised his chosen nation so it has become; Jewish people remain prosperous, full stop, period! Lucky had an old friend who was also his engineer and whom he referred to in all his album credits as "Rabbi." He is Jewish and according to what we have learnt, some Jewish people don't believe Jesus is their Messiah. But when faced with life-threatening incidents like bad turbulence, a riot at a show and so on, you would hear him say "Jesus!" and Lucky would say to him, "my Rasta but you don't believe in Him!"

Lucky never questioned whether Jesus Christ was the son of God he believed Jesus was sent specifically to the lost nation of Israel. What Lucky disconnected with was how we have now abandoned our beliefs to adopt the ways of others. He was an advocate of the things our forefathers believed in. Things he believed in still happen to this day, and by things I mean each one of us has an encounter at one point or another, an encounter unlike anything we've experienced before, that encounter we cannot make sense of except to acknowledge it as something divine. Whether we are born again or

55

not, Christian or not, Muslim or not Bhuddist or not, we all have these spiritual encounters. It is not like Lucky didn't want to move with times, but this forcing one another to believe in systems that don't resonate with us was something that irritated him. He believed God created the earth the way that he did and everyone in it belonged with the ways of his own people.

I remember in my early days at Gallo Record Company, Lucky had indicated in one of his interviews that not everyone who lived in Africa was African. This was one of the most criticised interviews he ever gave. Some people took it too personally. Some people hated him for it for evermore. I sit and wonder about it, or should I ask the question again: is everyone who lives in Africa African? I would like to know the answer myself. Perhaps this wasn't a politically correct statement at the time. But he paid for saying that, but he knew what he was saying. However, some will get it and some will never get it, never.

The only way to close this gap between poor scripture interpretation and the true meaning of scriptures is if we all partake in learning this will help us defend our own beliefs. Jewish people took their stance, God promised them certain things about their Messiah, the Jesus who came in a surprising manner could not have been what God promised them. To date they stand firmly on that promise for they know their standing with God. We all believe we're right, we all have strong enough reasons supporting our beliefs, some of which are biblical.

Google has to date recorded 20 major religions that are listed. They acknowledge the exact number is more than those listed because there are a lot of beliefs and religions all around the world. I think there are so many because everyone has their own interpretation; even the Bible has its own struggle. In fact, the Bible has to contend with more conflict than we humans! We all know that it was translated many times; it has many versions; it has lost meaning of certain events and hey! everyone claims to know what the proper meaning is supposed to be.

Lucky would raise issues of the earth and how it is uniquely made. "Rasta, do you think God wanted Indians to believe in the African stuff? Why didn't he create one big earth with everyone looking alike and having everything common?" he asked.

He believed God created the earth and everything in it for a reason, and we as a people argue about what each one of us should and should not be doing. He was a staunch African man who was not shaken by other cultures, practising his own culture fully. He made sure that other values didn't intrude in his own but rather embraced those values that complemented him.

He believed that if he went to his grandmother's grave to do what a man's got to do, that it was okay because that is his tradition. Why is it okay for some cultures to take flowers to graves but when we do the grave ritual the African way we are pagan, we are told our systems are pagan, nothing of ours is accepted, and we're also in agreement by stopping to doing what we were told is our tradition. These days it is common in South Africa to find wreaths on the side of the road, this to mark the spots where accidents took place and loved ones died. You wonder why certain people feel the need to do this disturbing thing, have they missed the very thing that my culture is able to address without the drama of wreaths and crosses on the side of the road? Perhaps we can learn from one another, to help with solutions to address these spiritual challenges. I am sure they don't lay these wreaths and crosses for no apparent reason, when you know you've buried your dearly departed why would you go back to that spot to lay a wreath, when the dearly departed has a grave. There are certain hidden things we cannot explain in life, where common sense doesn't apply, where no book affords answers, where nothing makes sense but we depend on the knowledge passed down to us by our elders and this knowledge is accessed through tapping or connecting spiritually, others will argue what connecting spirituality is supposed to be, we connect to God spiritually also.

We continue to argue about religion, the cause of religious wars, for what people? We travelled with Lucky and there were times he would say, I wonder if Christians who are in the plane know that most of the scientific inventions were made by non-believers, people who just believe in something beyond, something greater than what they can explain and yet they refrain from acknowledging that something as God. We believe God created everything that is, that was and that is still to come, He even gives that scientific idea to the one who doesn't believe or acknowledge Him to do something great. Why don't we boycott the boarding of an airplane if it was invented by someone who didn't believe in God, or refuse the hospital C-section if it was invented by a non-believer? What is important in life, I wonder. I am happy I crossed this spiritual path with Lucky Dube in my life, I have made my spiritual choices in life, I will no longer be intimidated by a system using the Bible to manipulate me.

He would tell me that before the Bible came to Africa our forefathers were in sync with the laws of nature and this being the case, did I believe that God and Jesus were new to Africans or that God loved us less? Or whether God only discovered us after the Bible was written. He made me realize that God was always there, that He is a simple father who requires of us to always do good, and understand the difference between good and evil. That God expects us to love Him more than we love ourselves and love our neighbours the way that we love ourselves. He said, "remember God is in control and we aren't. Love is the greatest command of them all, this thing called love."

God has been at work in our lives from the moment we were conceived. We are offered countless opportunities to draw nearer to Him, and at the time of God's choosing. But how do we draw nearer to Him with the heavy yokes the church has put on us, we can barely breath.

Lucky lived the better part of his life reading the scriptures and ensuring that others around him understood as well. What hurt him the most was seeing so many of our people being intimidated by their own, they use the very platform they should be using to set God's people free to further intimidate and use their own for their own personal gains. Some of the things he would point out were pertinent issues like setting aside the Sabbath as the Lord's day. He would argue that if God's people were confused between Saturday and Sunday why was it that those who worship on a Sunday don't set whole day aside? They would rather go to church for two hours and continue with their daily routine thereafter. And if church should take more than two hours, they'll complain as if a sin had been committed.

Another argument he had was about food mentioned in the Old Testament, things which God said should never be eaten. Lucky held that nowhere in the New Testament was it proclaimed that those foods can now be eaten. He would say if God was able to categorize these things in the Old Testament then what stops Him from qualifying them in the New Testament? The qualifying of eating of these foods is a rather vague assumption. God's people follow the masses without checking with their creator when they have the means to do it. The very people who introduced the Bible have been eating pork from time immemorial, and then they say doing certain African rituals like slaying an animal during a certain celebration is pagan. What does the Bible say about bacon? He simplified scripture in an amazing way. God knows the importance of giving your body a rest; He knows the reasons why we cannot eat certain foods, He made all of them and only He knows how bad they are for us to consume.

He would from time to time refer to our cultures and would mention that most of the poor people on earth are people without culture, if we learnt from the Jews and Indians who are not embarrassed by their own cultures, people would be spiritually and morally richer. We have adopted other cultures and this has robbed us of our blessings; the simple teachings of black people living in rural areas who are taught morals at early stages of their lives are able to display the same quality everywhere they go. Children of yesteryear were raised by the whole community; those children were morally

59

grounded for life. These are Lucky Dube's beliefs, his essence.

If we read the Bible ourselves a lot of truth would be revealed to us, he would say, but because we rely on some people to know and have a relationship with God we believe almost anything they tell us. He believed the Bible was the richest Book any historian could have written and continues to be the bestselling book of all time. Read it, We may not be able to understand everything we read in the Bible but the greatest reward of all is that God speaks to each and every one of us through the Bible. The teachers may teach us but what they teach is not always what God wants us to hear. There are huge gaps between what we are being taught, what others want us to know, and the truth. Once you start reading the Bible you get to understand why you should read it.

Lucky believed that if God loved him the way that He obviously did, he wanted to know Him more. He endeavored to seek wisdom from God; he had already sought God's kingdom and His righteousness but he still wanted more. When he prayed I didn't once hear him ask for more musical shows or wealth; he asked for wisdom, for him to be a good messenger. He already knew that God had taken care of the rest. He knew that God loved him too much, he was comfortable with God, never was afraid to tell the world about God. When someone did something good, he would ask God to bless them, always. This was what Lucky Dube believed in.

Lucky was realistic about deep issues, and inasmuch as I was shaken by this I continue to endeavour to know more about God and his beloved son Jesus Christ. I began to read the Bible like I read a novel and most of the things that have always been complicated in my life have been revealed, and most of it has been very scary.

I've also learned the difference between being religious and being spiritual. I prefer spirituality although I was brought up under a system of religion I've tasted both worlds. I now know the importance of having a relationship with my God without seeking a middle man. I read an article on the difference between religion and spirituality from the internet and although the origin is not that clear I found it very interesting and speaks to my experience having tasted religion and spirituality. The article in its original form was published on **September 29, 2010 from** <u>PreventDisease</u> **Website** <u>**Spanish version**</u>

It has become quite popular in recent years to distinguish between spirituality and religion.

It's true that there are valid distinctions between the two, but there are also a number of problematic distinctions which often and unnecessarily divide the two fields of thought.

One principal problem with attempts to separate religion from spirituality is that the former is saddled with everything negative while the latter is exalted with everything positive.

It is important to note the fact that many of the negative things which people attribute to religions are features of some forms of some <u>religions</u> (usually Judaism, Christianity, and Islam), but not of other religions (like Taoism or Buddhism).

Religion is spiritual and spirituality can also be considered religious. One tends to be more personal and private while the other tends to incorporate public rituals and organized doctrines.

The lines between one and the other may often not be clear or distinct depending on the interpretation.

Consider these definitions:

Religion is an institution established by man for various reasons. Exert control, instill morality, stroke egos, or whatever it does. Organized, structured religions all but remove god from the equation. You confess your sins to a clergy member, go to elaborate churches to worship, told what to pray and when to pray it. All those factors *remove you from god.*

Spirituality is born in a person and develops in the person. It may be kick started by a religion, or it may be kick started by a revelation. Spirituality extends to all facets of a person's life. *Spirituality is <u>chosen</u> while religion is often times <u>forced</u>.* Being spiritual to me is more important and better than being religious.

True spirituality is something that is found deep **within oneself**. It is your way of loving, accepting and relating to the world and people around you. It cannot be found in a church or by believing in a certain way.

Consider the following in favor of the spiritual path:

There is not one religion, but hundreds

There is only one type of spirituality

Religion is for those who want to continue rituals and the formality

Spirituality is for those who want to reach the Spiritual Ascent *<u>without</u> dogmas*

Religion is for those who are asleep

Spirituality is for those who are awake

Religion is for those that require guidance from others

Spirituality is for those that lend ears to their inner voice

Religion has a dogmatic and unquestionable assembly of rules that need to be followed without question

Spirituality invites you to reason it all, to question it all and to decide your actions and assume the consequences

Religion threatens and terrifies

Spirituality gives you inner peace

Religion speaks of sin and of fault

Spirituality encourages "living in the present" and not to feel remorse for which has already passed - Lift your spirit and learn from errors

Religion represses humanity, and returns us to a false paradigm

Spirituality transcends it all and makes you true to yourself

Religion is instilled from childhood, like the soup you do not you want to take

Spirituality is the food that you you seek, that satisfies you and is pleasant to the senses

Religion is not *God*

Spirituality is infinite consciousness and all that is - It is *God*

Religion invents

Spirituality discovers

Religion does not investigate and does not question

Spirituality questions everything

Religion is based on humanity, an organization with rules

Spirituality is DIVINE, WITHOUT rules

Religion is cause for division

Spirituality is cause for union

Religion seeks you so that you create

Spirituality causes you to seek

Religion continues the teachings of a sacred book

Spirituality seeks the sacredness in all the books

Religion is fed fear

Spirituality is fed confidence

Religion lives you in your thoughts

Spirituality lives in your conscience

Religion is in charge of the "to do"

Spirituality is in charge of the "to BE"

Religion is a dialectic

Spirituality is logic

Religion feeds the ego

Spirituality makes you transcend

Religion makes you renounce yourself to the world

Spirituality makes you live with *God*, not to renounce him

Religion is adoration

Spirituality is meditation

Religion is to continue adapting to the psychology of a template

Spirituality is individuality.

Religion dreams of glory and paradise

Spirituality makes you live it here and now

Religion lives in the past and in the future

Spirituality lives in the present, in the here and now

Religion lives in the confinement of your memory

Spirituality is LIBERTY in AWARENESS.

Religion believes in the eternal life

Spirituality makes you conscious of all that is

Religion gives you promises for the after-life

Spirituality gives you the light to find *God* in your inner self, in this life, in the present, in the here and the now...

May peace, happiness and universal love continue growing in your heart.

You are All That Is.

I have also admitted that the Bible was written and interpreted by man, that some of the situations interpreted may not be exactly what the authors meant as the original script. Some were interpreted few times before the final prints. I also understand that the different versions of the Bible differ in interpretation for whatever reason, and that I don't have to know everything. I shouldn't concern myself with the minor things of meaning and interpretation, God will take care of the things He wants me to know. So, whenever I feel confused and find it difficult to know what to believe, I can trust God to give me the wisdom to understand what He wants to show me. And as I learn more of God, He will give me the desire to live the way He teaches through the Bible. I have learned that He is the vine and I am the branch; I abide in God daily and God in me.

The ways of my forefathers are not documented in a huge book like the Bible, but I still believe it as it is told today; I believe those that still uphold the culture. When we are taught the things of God which are documented in the Bible, we believe what we are taught. We are asked to pray for our salvation, when no one in the Bible ever prayed for their salvation and we still believe we should do this. At times these church traditions are used to enslave us, they are used to hoodwink us to worship others, to let them oppress, intimidate, manipulate us into believing this is the will of God when it is man's will.

The whole Bible as I understand it is a very old book which contains ancient history about the beginning of creation and humanity and things that have happened and also things that are to come. My own understanding of the story of the Bible is about the Israelites. Some of us were not part of the story, but interestingly enough, we can believe it. For some the Bible has become the last thing they would want to associate with, for others it is their hope. It is the way it is, hope. I miss Lucky too much, it hurts. I started looking at the Bible differently he made it simple for me to look at it as literature, divine at that.

Lucky would engage me in Scripture any time of the day and he knew I would rise to the occasion with my Sunday school experience. We connected easily, as I have memories of the Sunday school verses in my head to this day. There were things that we agreed on and things we didn't. I remain thankful that I came into contact with the truth through association with a musician, in an industry where you would have thought there were all sorts of mischievous things! This shows that God is everywhere He is in all of us. This truth is one that has not divided what I believe in, this is the one truth that has liberated me. I made that choice not to let it divide me, I continue my journey knowing the truth, I can choose to stop believing in other things that were forced on me based on an informed decision or I can continue to build on the system, taking in what is working and leaving that which does not resonate with me. I have identified the things that the system used to control me when I was deprived of a freedom to think independently but now, I can never be brain washed by religion, no one can ever undermine my intelligence, no one can ever manipulate me, my mind is not sick and I do not need religion to cure it. Let us rid ourselves from this mental slavery and start thinking for ourselves. We are all in it together and if we are going to collectively find peace, freedom, justice, compassion, harmony, love that we all are in search of, we need spiritual solidarity to understand each other's views and beliefs, we are all together as one, God is part of us all. Again Lucky sang about it, I am hearing it in my heart, this time not just as music but my food for thought. My prayer is that my brothers and sisters should stop following religious teachings that get them to kill and harm each other in the name of God. We need to realize that religion is what it is, it has been successful in dividing nations. It is a strong system which we can all beat by asking the God that is supposed to be representing good why certain things happen to us. Surely He can do for us better than that which we have been told we deserve, better. Our God can do better for us.

I learnt a lot from Lucky and I know he learnt a lot from me. One of the lessons I won't lose is praying in my native language. He simply indicated that when you pray in English you battle to plead your case properly because you battle with words; when you pray, you pray from the heart, not from the head. I haven't even tried praying in English since this revelation. If your English is as basic as mine then it only makes sense to pray in your own language. God will hear you no matter what language you use.

There were times that Lucky would forget that we weren't at church and he would just want to talk about the Bible. God this, God that, this was kind of boring, for me, he would sound like a kid in a candy store or a kid who just received a new toy. He would call me for a meeting but once I got there he would even forget why we were meeting and just wanted to share what he was feeling at that time. He would share his experience of the past Sabbath when the preacher man asked him to preach on that day.

He would share with me: "Rasta, you've seen me perform with ease neh? "(neh is a local South African confirmation simply translated as "hey"), "but no one realizes how difficult it is to face so many people whilst singing and dancing; it's the most difficult thing anyone can do."

I disagree with him. The only time I've ever seen him different is a few minutes before he goes on stage. His mood switches and if you were to tell him that the show had been cancelled or he had to meet the Pope before the performance, he wouldn't hear you or understand anything you said. I suppose this is what he means by stage fright or being people shy. He never drank or smoked but a few minutes before he went on stage something would take over. He always took a moment to pray before he went on stage; after his prayer he wouldn't hear anything anyone said. He confirmed that he also didn't understand what took over at that moment. He would say, "Rasta, this is spiritual to me - you will not understand." He would admit there were certain things that he did on stage that he didn't understand himself. He would watch his performances on video and would not believe what he saw.

Lucky's shows in Africa were the biggest you could ever imagine. Not only did promoters compete in getting him to their shows, they obviously were making a killing out of them. I remember our last performance in Uganda when we had to leave the hotel at 10:00a.m for a late afternoon show to avoid traffic. The performance was due to happen around 18:00. What were we supposed to do to kill the hours in between?

Tickets had been sold out many days before the tour and the promoters wouldn't take a chance; we had to be there as early as possible. This was by the way the second show at the stadium, the first one the previous day was at the Nile Gardens. The first one is always a VIP event and the price was rather steep. I'm only getting it now, in retrospect. Lucky's purpose was clear; he was wealthy spiritually and that was enough for him. He was already comfortable in his life, God had blessed him in all areas and God's love and His grace were enough for him. He wouldn't ask for more than what God had already given him, and he was appreciative of what he was given. It was no longer the money he was making but the message he was bringing.

My journey with Lucky was based on a deep connection that was beyond what one can easily explain. He could 'sense' me from wherever he was, whether he was travelling or at his farm. Sometimes he would tell me what I wanted to say even before I could find the words. The phone would ring and he would just say what he had to say and leave me freaking out. He knew when I wasn't okay; if there was trouble in my life he knew it. He never short-changed anyone; he always made sure that he reached out to do what he could.

Strangely, when he travelled, the connection was even stronger. He would call and intervene in my situations, and thank goodness for that! I guess I have a lot of situations in my life – I always have had. He was there to assist when I couldn't handle my issues. I must confess, I sometimes tried to hide the truth but he was always spot on. I couldn't lie to Lucky over the phone, let alone face-to-face; he just looked into my eyes and knew. The only way I could lie to him was in writing, but even then … A part of me hated this ability of his; I thought he was invading my private space. It's funny that I thought of it that way, because he wasn't spying on me or interfering; there was just this thing that he had that I cannotexplain, and I didn't really get it until now.

One day I walked into his office and he told me I had come in with a very strong energy. He confirmed it was good energy though, but that he couldn't handle it. I thought he was going bananas, but I told him I wasn't hearing this for the first time. I hear it all the time, actually, but the problem is that I never bother to ask what people mean. I still don't. I hope one day someone will explain this to me but I'm afraid to ask in case they offend me! I would rather just be told without inviting it.

I lost my dear mother through a terrible crime in October of 2005. For quite a while I tried to hide how badly the trauma had affected me. I hid it from many people, but not from Lucky. Every time I was deeply emotional he felt it, and would call in the middle of the night to say all would be well. He would call during the day to assure me that eventually it would get better and I would be fine. Below is part of an email he wrote to me in May of 2006:

Lucky Dube <luckydube@icon.co.za> wrote:

We normally do our evening prayer at 6, but in winter it would be anytime from 4;30.

Today we started at about 5;13. Throughout the whole session I was thinking about you, and I worry because at that time, nothing should be in my mind just the word of God. This got me scared, now I wonder if you are okay, is something troubling you what is? Okay just checking ... this strange sadness.

Wednesday, 24 May, 2006 11:12

From: "lenah mochoele" <mochoele@yahoo.

To: "Lucky Dube" luckydube@icon.co.za

Rasta

70

Thanks for the email, you never cease to amaze me. I went to see my brother on Sunday, and then I went home yesterday to go and check if things were still okay at my mom's house. But the reason I did all this was that I hit rock bottom emotionally the past weekend. And then you wrote to me on Monday and I only see your email today.

I thought perhaps going home and going to see my brother would bring me some peace. The past weekend was exactly a year after I had taken my mother to my brother in Rustenburg. But whilst I was at home yesterday I thought let me go and check how far the cops were with the case I asked to see the file and I saw the pictures that were taken by forensic. Yesterday was okay I was strong and all but today I am something else, well this whole morning felt like the 2nd October 2005. I just wish I could have some closure of this chapter in my life so I can carry on with my life. It has been very difficult, I've been thru stuff in my life but nothing as complicated as this. The problem is that I keep on having these dreams about her, I know I am not supposed to speak to her in my dreams but I have been able to. Sometimes she refuses to speak to me but I insist she does. I think this is my problem. I don't know what this means. I wish I knew. I will come with you guys to Nelspruit. Thanks.

The day that my mother was murdered I had a terrible dream. I dreamt I had been bitten by a neighbor's dog, and the bite was terribly painful – it felt real and strong. I've always been able to make a plan to get out of trouble in my dreams but this time I couldn't. I remember it was a puppy, not a big dog, but it wouldn't let go of my hand. It bit me severely, so when the call came that morning that I must come home and that my mother was ill, I knew it was more than that, that something terrible must have happened.

I have a history of scary dreams and most of them came to pass. As a result I decided to keep the dreams to myself in case people suspected me of being the one causing the problems. I shared some of my dreams with Lucky and he encouraged me to tell them anyway. But I still can't bring myself to do that.

71

I must confess, though, that I never fully acknowledged the kind of connection we had then, but I have come to appreciate it now that he's gone. My journey with Lucky made me aware that we are connected with others; it made me re-discover and re-commit to my life's purpose. I've come to the conclusion that people meet and interact for a reason; I have this incredible feeling desire to continue his legacy. It can't be that we simply met, worked together, spent a lot of quality time together, and he then just died. That is superficial, whereas what we shared was profound and dynamic. It can't be that he just chose to tell me the things he did for no apparent reason, or maybe it was innocent, I don't know. But I thinkmy journey with him has a deeper meaning than that, and I need to reach out and discover the purpose of the journey. Now that he's gone I have learned to be self-aware. I am conscious of my surroundings, the way I reason, the way I relate to those around me, and even the way I walk. Itis as if he has set me a constant reminder, so I would not forget. I came to understand that connecting with others spiritually is important and should not be ignored, for there are reasons why we need to connect. When he did his shows Lucky always made sure he was wired correctly so his atmosphere could tune in easily. When he travelled he made sure his wires were up to date, when he did his interviews and all his engagements, he would ensure his connections were right. He would tell you if he didn't want to be in the company of certain individuals, if it doesn't feel right he would not do it.

There is this thing that I thought was profound about the Lucky crowds. I began to understand that Lucky didn't have fans but rather he had followers, who were not ignorant. His followers shared his message and were committed to following him in his journey through his music. Lucky's followers knew what he stood for; they knew him. They remained true to themselves and didn't lose themselves to anything. It didn't matter how big the shows were, they were all peaceful. There were times when he would stop a show just to ask the law enforcements to stop harassing people, and they would listen and the shows would go on peacefully. Sometimes he would even say the law enforcements were the ones causing trouble, because they needed to show off their powers. At times you would find law enforcements in the crowds themselves having forgotten that they were on duty. He loved the crowds as if he knew them personally, and this because Lucky took time to connect, yes, connect before he went on stage, I was there, I experienced it, I may not have known what it was, but I know now. He did not take advantage of the stage, that he is the most powerful thing when on stage, he connected spiritually with the crowds, they gave him what he needed, he shared what he needed to share in the most serene, peaceful and respective atmosphere one would have ever expected.

Today because of Lucky Dube I read my Bible with a conviction. I will not go to the gospels for my marching orders. The law was not given to me. I was not a lost nation, God never wanted for my ancestors to be a special people to Him. He chose one nation, a nation that He Himself said I should learn from to observe these things. I have been to many places in my life, never have I been to myself. If the Bible is a book written by people who God appointed to account for the things that happened with the one nation, where is my story, He chose for the other story to be told, it was within His right to do so. My story may not have been documented in that big book that we all argue as to what it should be when it's not even our own story but it is there. When he realised it, Lucky Dube went for it. We do not have to practice to be Jews, we can go into their history to learn their history, which we were also commanded to observe. I love the way the gospels according Matthew ends, divine. I have learnt from it that Jesus Christ came at His first advent for the sake of the Jew, that's the reason why I understand that certain things are meant for certain people to adhere to and not me, lest I get them wrong and offend God. I have my own rich culture which did not make it into the Bible, a culture I connect with, which I am supposed to adhere to her moral codes, this culture which religion tried to erase from my heart, I am willing to engrave in my heart. And nobody will ever, take away from my people.

I travelled to many places with Lucky, I have experienced a lot of things in the process. There are people in this world who still uphold their cultures and there were times when he himself would admire such people. Sometimes you would wish nobody finds them, for selfish reasons of course, you would want to protect them from these pollution of religion. Their cultures are so admirable. Life is sacred, uncomplicated and you can see God in these people. These areas are where everyone wants to go, you wonder why? Some people plan every year to visit these places just to go and connect with themselves, for in these areas there are great energies that one draws peace from.

My exodus without Lucky has awakened in me great spiritual truths, I've discovered a lot of Biblical truths. My next prayer is:

Dear God

Thank you for the opportunity you afforded me to meet Lucky Dube, as I continue my journey here on earth please help me to discern more.

Amen

3. PURPOSE-DRIVEN LIFE

We had included Eugene Mthethwa in the memorial service program at the Baseline to speak on behalf of friends and one of the people who had worked with Lucky as a keyboard player. Eugene is one of the most seasoned musicians in the South African music industry. I must have met Eugene at the same time as I met Lucky Dube at Gallo, although at the time he had moved on in his musical career with a popular kwaito band Trompies. The South African music industry boasts a good number of professional disciplined musicians and Eugene is one of those that have survived the industry amidst the pressures that come with being in the public eye. The pressures of being famous can affect musicians negatively, its celebrity effects are detrimental and many musicians have not been able to survive the pressures. It is difficult to survive the red carpets, the glitz the glamour, and all of the other blinding celebrity syndromes of our industry. For Eugene fortunately he is one of the few disciplined and level headed ones, at his age I admire him for having survived this vicious business. I was deeply moved by the speech he delivered during the memorial service, where multitudes had gathered and crowded the venue to remember Lucky Dube. We have had to erect large screens outside as the venue could not accommodate everyone. When Eugene came on stage to speak to the legacy of Lucky Dube, his resounding speech captivated my heart. It confirmed one thing, Lucky had been consistent in his career, Eugene had known Lucky many years before I met him but everything he said about Lucky was everything I personally got to know about him too. This is what he had to say about Lucky (original script)...

"The Dube family, the political leadership, friends and colleagues, the congregation at large, all protocols observed, I greet you all in the name of the most high.

I believe every situation presents a lesson to be taken home, and that is the issue of vision and purpose that Lucky embraced above identity.

If I were to ask Lucky Dube today to choose between celebrity status or to live the purpose of his life, he would have chosen the purpose [rather] than the status.

If it were not for his music he wouldn't have gone out of his way to find an alternative way of becoming a public figure, and therefore in all what we do today and what will happen on Sunday, let us afford him and his family that privacy, that we anyway voluntarily afforded him whilst he was still alive.

Democracy is not a "one size fits all" but it requires a society to shape it according to its cultural values and norms, thus my call today, is to revisit our African values that constitute "ubuntu."

All the arrangements made by the family are purpose-driven to the fulfilment of Lucky Dube's values and norms. I therefore urge all of us to respect in the manner that would suit Lucky's philosophical reasoning.

Lucky wrote and sang songs against many situations that are happening today, even long before 1994.

Songs like "Little heroes" that talks about how abortion is so cruel to the unborn babies who go down the drains day by day, how they cry out so loud, but the whole world is not listening, only the mothers of the world can save the children for they have no political organisation to fight for their rights.

He wrote "Together as one" and "Different colours, one people" even before Mandela could speak of a rainbow nation.

He sang about Group Areas Act going, Apartheid going and made those who instituted Group Areas Act and Apartheid to dance to such lyrics, as I indicated in my letter about the sad performance we

76

had in Namibia whilst apartheid was still rife.

He wrote against women and children abuse through the song called, "I am a slave," a liquor slave who traumatises wife and child who know that every day there's double trouble coming home.

He was a visionary and a prophetic writer, thus he clearly captured the end of his life in the song called, "Crime and corruption."

All he wanted was to send a message, whether it was accepted or not; he didn't care because he had a vision and a purpose-driven life.

Many of us are living fake lives that are empty with no fulfilment because we get carried away by the continuous search for identity; you know the "they must see me" syndrome (that I am a celebrity – can you really celebrate yourself?)

I live in a mansion – it's not yours but the bank's until you pay it up in 20 years if you would still be acting your role in generations or writing hits for that matter.

Look at me – I drive a hummer ... liar, it's the bank's or maybe it is even leased.

If I were to take you through the question of identity, that we so embrace, you would walk out of this place confused and doubting even your own identity because it is not what we physically see of you, be it your body or your face, these could be altered in an accident but post the accident you don't change from being you, or when you die, you continue living through memories.

Even if scientifically they could feed the computer with identical memories that you have, it does not change the computer to be you.

One would maybe think that it is the mind that carries all the information about you, that makes you you, but even if you could turn into a vegetable today, you would remain the same person you

77

were before the incident.

The only thing left would be to say, maybe you are a soul, but again the soul is not physical, how would one identify it, how would one say this is the same soul that I saw yesterday. Where is the soul situated in your body?

So let us not be consumed by these socially constructed identities and values but concentrate on finding things that when we do, would give us that fulfilment and the ultimate happiness in the absence of pain; not drugs certainly, cause they ultimately bring pain. Remember the TK and Brenda Fassie incidents.

Those who love reading please go read about utilitarianism as a moral philosophical subject, then you will understand the desire and the vision that Lucky Dube had, for ordinary South Africans and the country as a whole.

He wouldn't have been impressed to see this whole opportunistic hype about crime, and the criticism of government only when crime hits people like him.

But he would have been more happy to see similar treatment given to those ordinary South Africans who die every day unnoticed because they are not celebrities.

We are all either accessories or acquaintances to crime. How many of us have members of our families involved in heists and robberies but we don't report them? How many artists have disclosed their drug addiction but none have exposed the suppliers in order to prevent them from supplying this deadly substance to other potential clients who are also our brothers and sisters? Let us rather take a collective responsibility and contribute towards a change. Criminals are from our own communities and not from the government.

Lucky, may your soul rest in peace. Indeed, you ran your race with dignity and pride, and you made many of us better men and women

78

due to the education that we wouldn't have received from school,
but by travelling around the world with you, I salute you! Aluta
continua!"

From: Eugene Mthethwa, On behalf of friends

What a divine testimony by Eugene, I am certain that he must have
been proud to bring to the spotlight aspects of a character many
thought was a musician just like any other. Continue to discern
Eugene for in you lies the qualities of a great leader. May God
continue to bless you. Lucky Dube placed the values of integrity on
his beliefs. We see this truth in his songs, which centre mainly on
social and personal issues; he hated racism, tribalism, corruption,
injustice, oppression, tyranny and exploitation. His music is riddled
with the desire to make the world a better place for everyone. His
main purpose in life was clear – firstly, to please God and secondly,
to make this world a better place. He preached about love, he had
faith, he never stepped out of his calling. When his earlier work as a
young musician didn't yield the expected desires he didn't give up;
something in his heart told him to go on – he endured. He worked
outside of the system; he was not a professional this or that; what he
had was passion in his heart, a burning desire. This burning passion
saw him speak to God's children all over the world; his was a
different address. He entertained, while at the same time preaching
messages of peace and unity; he believed if he carried on with his
message of encouraging others not to give up, that one day things
would change for the better.

He told a story when he was still alive and his story came from
having a purpose-driven life. Lucky Dube knew why he was on
earth; he told his story in what he did and said, he lived his purpose.
Billy Domingo, who tour-managed most of Lucky's African gigs,
and I, developed a habit of disappearing after we checked Lucky
into his hotel room. He never stopped telling his story, he would tell
it with every breath he took. He would not let you go until he
finished his line; sometimes this line was too long and we would
lose concentration. But he knew he had to tell his story before he

could depart this earth. He didn't have to leave this earth to leave a legacy; his legacy was his purpose-driven life which he expressed through his music. He expressed his purpose by word and action; if he preached about something you must know that he practised it too. Lucky's success was not achieved in one day. He worked very hard to get the world to listen to him; and when it finally did, the audiences gave him attention in return. They listened and they watched and followed because they couldn't ignore the story. He sang from his heart and his listeners could hear it resounding in their own hearts. Billy and me listened to the story from the horse's mouth every time we were on the road with him; the story was very long and sometimes too painful to listen to. Some of the wisdom he shared with us was that we were sent here for a specific reason, that each and every one of us on earth had a divine mission that we needed to accomplish before we die. He would say, "look around you, do you believe that everything that is around you is the way that it is supposed to be, or do you believe it is just there?"

I would disagree with him when we had bad days, like the time when we spent Christmas at Heathrow Airport because we had missed our flight back to South Africa … how can God allow me to sleep at the airport when I should be home with my kids in warm South Africa? When you've planned your travel knowing when and how you would get back home on time, and then Sierra Leone Airline cancels the flight that connects you to the last flight to South Africa on 24 December 2002, how exactly is this 'the way it is supposed to be'? Does this make sense? No it doesn't, it is just bad planning on the part of the airlines, period!

I think I've driven a strong point home. When he doesn't give up he goes on to show me what other things might be awaiting not only me but those I'm with. This level of spirituality is too much for me to comprehend; "It is not always about you, my Rasta, God is in charge, we are not. So my Rasta, next time when something like this happens, when you don't understand why things are the way they are, it's time to yield and let God be. He certainly knows what He's doing all the time. It's all in the master plan! God is not a genie...

He is He Who He Is, God. You can be the best planner and have all the money in the world but the buck stops with God; if He says yes then it will be done, period."

I imagine if we all had to change the way we think about the situations in our lives, how far we could go! People wouldn't yell at others because they've been wronged; people wouldn't hate others for whatever spurious reasons they come up with; there would be no resentment, blame and all the other stuff that we go through every day. We would all have a better understanding of situations and we would be more tolerant of one another, understanding that none of us is perfect, permanent and complete. We would understand that the person next to me might have been sent to me to change a very bad situation in my life to something very good, or to add some value to my empty life. We would understand our essential purpose of coming to this earth to make it a better place, contribute our part to the human race and go back to our Creator, instead of us concentrating on earthly desires and possessions! We would stop yelling and screaming all the time, as if our yelling and screaming could change the situation we are in, anyhow. We live in an era that unfortunately seeks to control us as if we were brainless, born less than human, and deserve less than what God intended for us.

Our generation is spiritually dead. We don't know who we are, what we're here for or where we're heading. Lucky Dube worked against a system that was designed to control others, a system designed to foster a certain dependency on it so that people cannot think for themselves. His messages sought to address these issues. He knew what the consequences of such a robbing system were; he asked us to join him in fighting this in his song Crime and Corruption. Since he died as a result of crime, would you join me now in fighting it? Do you ever worry about leaving home in the morning and coming back in a coffin in the evening? And how long are you going to keep criminals from breaking into your home, even with the best security system? How long are you going to keep them from taking your car? Those who killed Lucky were dead already – they were dead spiritually. They were born to dead parents. I don't even blame them because most of us are dead without realising it. Our parents were molded by a system and robbed of their humanity and originality, and I don't even want to touch on their God-given land and its riches. Our parents had to conform to the patterns of this world to fit in and they had no choice, they had to survive.

Fortunately, our generation doesn't have to and this is what Lucky was preaching about; change your mindset and rely on the Almighty. Your eyes will be opened and you'll gain God's wisdom. Those dead people who killed Lucky for whatever reason, mean so little that there is no need to even know why they killed him. We can only pray that they see the light at the end of the day, we pray for their discernment wherever they are. Discern, for your light has come.

DISCERN AND SHINE (poem)

Let there be light discern and shine

For your light has come

Your time has come Africa

To stop the destruction within your borders

Discern Africa and shine

Yesterday the glory of Jah was upon you

Today darkness covers the land

Discern and shine Africa

Let the goodness of Jah be felt

In this land of hope

The land of our forefathers

Discern arise and shine Africa

For your light has come

The enemy is standing aside and looking

As we slash and kill our own brothers

Discern my Africa discern

Let nations stream to your light

Africa my hope discern

The darkness that covers the land

Shall be no more

Discern Africa my Zion

Violence will no more be heard in your land

Ruin or destruction within your borders

Discern mother and feed the children

Discern father and protect the children

Discern brother and bring honour to your father

Discern sister and bring joy to your mother

Discern son, this is your future

Discern daughter and nurture Africa

Discern my Africa, the land of my forefathers

The light of the world has blinded us

Arise and shine for your light has come

The light of the most high, Jah the Almighty

The sun will no more be your light by day

Jah will be your everlasting light

Discern motherland discern

Discern for your light has come

Bring back my dignity from yesterday

Bring back my courage from yesterday

Bring back my hope from yesterday

Bring back my joy from yesterday

Bring back my pride from yesterday

Bring back my wisdom from yesterday

Bring back my praise from yesterday

Discern my Africa for your light has come

Discern and don't trust your heart alone

For it is deceitful at times

Discern and seek counsel with the wise

Discern and run away from the wicked

Discern and listen to the voice of Jah

Discern and take it to Jah

Discern and answer this

Who are you Africa

Where do you come from Africa

Where are you Africa

Where are you going Africa

Discern and answer this

What is your name Africa

What is the name of your father Africa

Africa I say discern and answer this

I say what is the name of your mother Africa

Discern and answer me Africa

What is the name of your grand father

That wise one who lived over the hills

Discern Africa and answer this

What is the name of your grandmother Africa

The one who cooked herbs to heal the children

Children of a great promise

Equipped skillfully by nature

Blessed divinely by her ancestors

Discern and shine for your light has come

To acknowledge your gifts

To acknowledge your talents

Passed down from generations

Discern Africa for your light has come

Discern and shine for your time has come

Discern and shine for your light has come Africa

I hear wisdom crying in the street

Wisdom pleading and pleading and pleading

And you are not listening Africa

And you will not hear Africa

Discern for I hear wisdom crying louder now

I hear wisdom calling Africa names

I hear her say you are naive Africa

I also hear her say you are fools Africa

Discern Africa for I myself am ashamed

At wisdom calling us names

Discern and shine for your light has come

Lucky always knew that the things of this earth are temporary; he was hoping that one day the leaders of the world would get this understanding. In his song Taxman he warns us to remember that the same people whom we've put in power, will change their tune and turn against us. Lucky didn't die in vain – the things he'd been preaching about are now coming to pass. I'm sure his soul will rest in peace one day. Now we know why Lucky's dollar wasn't strong enough to keep criminals off the streets. Some of our taxes are being used for unnecessary luxuries. But he preached about it and the reason they hated him was because he exposed them. Who can disagree with him today?

Standing out from his peers from early days, Lucky knew who he was and never tried to fit in with the crowd. He never had to go and steal, rob and do bad things. I remember seeing him tired after a hard day's work, never complaining but being proud and grateful that he'd brought something home so that his family could eat and survive. He told me the lovely story of his grandmother being a magician. "Rasta, my gogo," (grandmother in Zulu) "would cook one potato and she would be able to feed ten children! We would all go to bed on full stomachs, and I mean full, from the one potato."

If he should buy himself a new car, it wouldn't be because he wanted to fit in with a certain class, he simply could afford to buy it and pay for it. He would never be pressured to own this or that just because he could afford to take a loan from the bank. In fact, he never took loans to pay for anything. He stood out because he had immense presence, not because he wore fashionable clothing, or expensive shoes, jewellery and all of the other things the human heart desires. His was a simple life lived with a purpose, with one mission: love for humankind. He never pretended to come from a wealthy family when he became famous; he always remembered the sacrifices his grandmother had made, going to bed on a grumbling stomach just so the children could have full tummies. He was never embarrassed to tell the story of his poor origins for fear of losing respect from others. This was the story of his life and he wasn't going to forget it; this was his history.

While many of us spend our precious time doing absolutely nothing to make a difference in life, he spent his writing songs that gave others hope, songs of love, songs of encouragement and peace. As if he had been told to do it now, as if he knew that we are in this world but temporarily. Having spent time with Lucky personally, I can confirm that he wasn't into material things. He bought a good car because it was a necessity. Something that will always stay in my heart is what Lucky's wife said during one of our conversations. Sobbing, she said, "you know, I wish it was possible to buy a person back from the dead! If this was possible, I'm sure Lucky would be happy if we sold everything that we owned and went and lived in a shack … because those criminals don't understand that Lucky never cared about material things, and yet he was killed for his possessions."

The things that he had, he had to sweat hard for (ask me, because after each performance I would wrap his stage clothes in towels as they would be soaking wet!). Lucky worked hard for his money, but others believe you can just use a gun to get anything you want. After hearing how many crimes those criminals committed the same week they killed Lucky, one really wonders if their needs exceeded what they got from their criminal acts in just that week. If Lucky couldn't afford something, he wouldn't buy it; he would wait and save for it and then buy it. He was very thoughtful about the future of his children and made provision for his family. It makes me mad to think that some of my tax money is used to feed and support these criminal bastards in jail.

I suppose people will wonder why I'm writing this story … I'm not related to Lucky and he's been gone for a few years now. But I knew the man well and he had a really positive impact on my life. And I also know that he touched many other hearts as well.

As time has passed, the urge to record his life and teachings has become too powerful for me to ignore. I feel others need to know that we have people who are successful today because they've been loyal to the human cause. I needed to tell Lucky's part of the story that he himself would never have been able to tell. A part of me has been taken away; as for many of Lucky's family, friends and fans, the world was a better place with Lucky in it. Now that we've lost his wisdom, I need to bring him closer to those fans who never understood who he was, outside of what they could hear and read. He was called according to God's purpose, he played his role in our lives, and then he had to move on. Difficult as it is to write this part, if he were alive he would joke about it and say, "okay, my Rasta, do you want to play God? Don't you know that He's in control? Do you think if He wanted me saved He wouldn't have done it? He loves me too much ... I have no doubt, God is Who He is, He doesn't report to me, I report to Him. And you know Rasta, when He called me by my name I answered. Do you know that? But hey, Rasta – the suckers gave me a fright, that's why I had to drive on after they shot me!" I keep imagining his last moment, what it was like. I know one thing though ... that through it all God was there, He was there all the time.

As people we always concern ourselves with the things we can't control; others even include or exclude God in the things that we don't understand. We are only human so we're supposed to act humanly. Lucky, himself, through his song "Put a little love" asked why bad things happen to good people. But he wasn't questioning why God allows these things. We simply have to yield during these moments. But I'm wiser now; I don't have to understand everything. Instead, I take everything to God.

Lucky requested to be buried in the most simple way possible. He believed that we came from dust and to dust we will return. He used to preach about people who used funerals as a platform to show how much they can afford. A funeral is a send-off to dust and people seem to invest in very expensive caskets to show off. The price of these things is often far more than they ever allowed the deceased to enjoy while they were still alive.

He would say, "Rasta, I don't know whether this is stupidity or ignorance but why would anyone buy a R30 000 casket that is going to waste? It's like taking R30 000 and burying it in the soil! This money could be used for the poor – or better causes. The things that Lucky used to talk about sometimes really scared me. If we say that we're giving someone a decent burial when the person next door can't afford to educate their child, are we being realistic? If someone worked hard during their life, does it mean vast amounts should be spent on an expensive casket?

"Why do we invest in funerals?" Lucky said. "When I die, Rasta, I want to be buried in a traditional coffin that costs nobody anything. It will cost those that make it some time and that's all – or maybe a few cuts," he joked.

It is worrisome that these days even the poorest of the poor try to match the standards of those who have money; funerals are becoming a platform to show off. And after all the traditional festivities and mountains of food, the family is left with debt to settle; sometimes huge debt. Do we put each other under this unnecessary pressure so that we can keep up with the Shabalalas, or is it just human nature that we also want to be talked about after the funeral? Whether you are in a casket or wrapped in cloth, you will return to dust, period. I battle with this a lot. I have tried to put myself in this situation and imagined my children at my funeral, feeling the pain and the shame. I wonder if the quality of my coffin will add more pain to them sending me off that way. I wonder if I would want them to use the money they would have wasted on an expensive casket differently and wisely. I also wonder about what my friends would think about me after this … I'm only wondering. When my mom died I had to upgrade her coffin for a better one. Poor soul had been paying an undertaker a monthly fee towards her burial. I personally don't have a fraction of the money Lucky Dube had and yet I had to upgrade my mom's coffin. My mother, that plain old lady, who just loved her community and her church until death did them part. That beautiful, short lady who raised me in that same community. And yet, she too was murdered; the reason why still remains a mystery. I had to upgrade her coffin and in ordinary, surface terms, I don't know why I felt it was necessary. Perhaps it was to ease the indescribable pain I felt when I found her lying murdered in her bed that Sunday morning. But this is a story for another day.

So Lucky Dube was unpretentious enough to be sent off in a handmade coffin, practically no money spent on it; and here we are today, talking about expensive caskets for people who can ill afford them. Why is it that we, who do not matter, worry about status and agonise about what people might say about us? Do we live for others or do we live for God? We worry about whether there will be enough people at the funeral, we worry about the quality of the coffin, we worry about the type of food we serve the multitudes, half of whom we don't even know.

My journey with Lucky has awakened in me great spiritual truths. It is true if one changes the way one thinks, more especially socially, it broadens the way you perceive life and there's nothing as fulfilling as being content, knowing you have no pressures from life. Lucky had no pressures; he was just himself, living his life for the Lord.

As a little girl I remember how proud I used to be, being the first one to find a chapter that the preacher man suggested every Sunday. I knew my Bible! Part of my journey's provision today is that understanding of the composition of the Bible: when the different books were written and why, or for whom. It helps when it comes to referring to a particular book or scripture, as well as understanding that history repeats itself. I must admit it wasn't easy, as a child, during my Sunday school days. There was never a break to play with the other kids. Monday to Friday was normal school, half of Saturday was spent on choir practice, and Sunday was church. If all of this could earn me straight ticket to eternal heaven, it was hard work, but worth it!.

I woke up one day and realized that I had one of the rarest opportunities to learn the divine mysteries of God through someone who came into my life for a very short while. He was called to be with the Lord when we least expected it. There is a saying that no-one is indispensable, but I beg to differ on that notion. There are people you can never replace inlife. Isn't it time for us to understand that some of our religious and spiritual leaders' teachings are limited, and that each and every one of us has a responsibility to read the Bible for ourselves? The choosing of certain beliefs is a personal thing, although most of the time it's done on the pretext that it is the right thing, or a better choice than 'this or that.' As I continue the journey, I want to learn more about this wonderful God who called me by my name before I was conceived. I wanna know Him from where I am sitting, at my level, no influence from the world. It is just Him and I. A God who causes all things to work together for good for those who love Him. My journey is that of understanding that God predestined my life to be able to serve Him, but how could I have been able to serve Him when I was instructed how toserve Him, where and when. As if He Himself had not commanded us to do these things.

We are blessed today because God is raising some great teachers of His word who are anointed and who are able to simplify the complex spiritual truths. Very few are able to share the big picture. Some of them have spent years behind the scenes attempting to unravel the truth. Although some pastors gloss over the heavy stuff for fear of losing their congregations, others are discerning at the same time. There are so many of these congregations that it becomes very easy for anyone to walk into a church and hear things that will make them feel good. And when it feels good, that's when people will stay, church also knows this, that's why they give the messages they give. Church is regarded as an institution that will be there to pray for you when things are really bad. I guess church is a place you find people who have had many issues in life, we go to church for help, not to worship God but to look for solutions.

The lighter side of Lucky – an amazing side – was his effortless humor. He used his humor to cover up his shyness, to avoid attention, and to charm those around him, both male and female. Once you were touched by his humor bug you were won over for life, and people were amazed at his personality outside of the stage. His story was long enough to keep telling it, even if it meant he was doing this to avoid attention. People loved taking pictures of him but he wouldn't allow anyone to take a photo of just himself. He never refused anyone who wanted to pose with him in a photo; he believed pictures are meant for memories and if you took a picture of just him it had no significance. In hindsight, I think he knew that his days to complete his mission on this earth were numbered. I am sure the many people who had theirpictures taken with him do understand today. There were so many people whom we met at airports, in the streets, hotels, and so on; they now have a good memory and a story to tell. The story they tell is that Lucky refused to let me take his picture alone, and insisted that I be in the picture. What a beautiful story!

His shows weren't always perfect but he always thanked God anyway. One of his songs, Rasta Man's Prayer which he wrote many years ago, goes like this:

There comes a time

In every man's life he's got to face

The truth, no matter what

We are coming to you, Father

With our sins and everything

To thank you

Those that smoke marijuana

Wanna thank you, Father

For making it grow internationally

They wanna thank you, Lord

Even though police cut it down

Sometimes they burn it down

But it grows again

Thank you, Father

We wanna thank you, Father

For everything you've given us

Nations that oppress other nations

Wanna thank you, Father

Even though it's painful to the oppressed

But they thank you…

For making them strong

Politicians wanna thank you, Father

For making them to be able

To lie with a straight face

While the nation cries

They wanna thank you, Lord

Looking back, I realise how tremendously fun-loving, as well as wise, he was. He served a God of laughter, with a sense of humour; a God of Love, a God of understanding, a God of grace and mercy. He knew you didn't need to be uptight with God. If he was confronted with a challenge he would take a moment to be on his own with his God; he would call it 'consultation time'. Let me go find out what God says about this situation, he would say. Sometimes I would ask curiously, "so what did God say?" He would reply, "He hasn't answered yet, but watch this space ...".

He had no time for worries. He was fearless throughout his journey. He was powerful, lovely and sober. No situation was too big for God to handle, he would assure me, saying that God was always talking to us but we often chose not to listen, or to ignore Him. Proverbs 3:6 was a favourite: "In all thy ways acknowledge Him, and He shall direct Thy paths." I feel obligated to share my journey which will remain a blessing for me until the end of time. I know Lucky shared time with others, but he chose to share his spiritual life with very few people, and I am so blessed to know that that includes me. I saw him joke with some, discuss sports with others, argue about politics with different people, but he wouldn't mix issues in his life.

If we think of Life as a journey, we know we need provisions and we need a plan. We need to pack our bags, taking everything we'll need along the way, armouring ourselves spiritually. Once we know our true values, we can't be brain-washed or believe everything others tell us. God will reveal to us certain things which are not visible to others.

4. AN ADVOCATE OF ORDER

There is no doubt that Lucky Dube had many gifts.

He was consistent in his messages, as if he was prophesying. He sang about religion and South African politics and world problems, but underlying everything, this theme was about order. He said in most of his songs that problems would be solved by the people themselves. What did he mean by that? If we could change our mindsets about what we want to see happen in our societies, it would be a huge first step. We allow wrong things to happen and when we're affected we cry foul. We are a complacent nation who worships those in leadership positions. We are comfortable accepting wrong things as long as they benefit us. The true South Africa for all, non-racial and non–sexist, would be an orderly Utopia. If we were orderly, we wouldn't accept the things that happen in our society today; if we received proper orders from our leaders the world would be a different place.

In today's terms, it's who you serve and not the cause, instead of the reverse. In the process of not having and keeping order, we leave room for others to compose songs such as Taxman. Lucky lays it open in his song; questions what the Taxman does with his money when there's still so much suffering, We're still asking why the majority of South Africans don't have decent jobs, houses and basic services. He questions what government does with his tax money when there are so many crimes committed on the streets. He emphasises that he pays his gardener to do his garden, but his tax money doesn't seem good enough for government to cover the services that they are supposed to cover. Again, who is to blame in all of this – the leaders or ourselves? If we kept our country in order, the many frustrated South Africans, some of whom sacrificed everything and went into exile, wouldn't be kicked out of the system today. Good people are being destroyed by their own brothers and sisters and we sit back and do nothing because we've forgotten where we came from. If Lucky was still alive, I promise you they would be blaming him for causing some of these nyakafater (street language for senseless) happenings in our country. But before I leave this part of my story, I would like to dedicate one of Lucky's songs to my government, lest you forget Lucky's prophecy, Guns and Roses, which Lucky wrote five years after our democracy.

I don't know why

I keep believing

That one day, they'll bring us together

When they've shown

In more ways than one

That all they care about is the dollar

I sit and wonder what this song would mean to some of our leaders today, what it meant then when it was sung for the first time, and the meanings this song would have in the many years to come. I sit and wonder what Lucky had seen for him to have written a song like this, and what he knew would be in the future. I am just wondering.

You belong to the one political party

I belong to the one musical party

Our differences are worlds apart

Just like guns and roses

If we don't take control

Of the situation

We'll stay forever in this ya commotion

As I sit and wonder where these guns and roses are taking us, I

wonder if it will come to an end one day.

Let me repeat what Lucky said in the guns and roses of our

time, with my own addition in bold:

How can five years of power

Destroy a lifetime of

Togetherness

And make a request to my leaders:

Let us take control of the situation

Otherwise we'll be trapped in this yacomotion

Without ignoring the fact that these guns and roses are a legacy of Apartheid, I honestly do not wish to see our children trapped in these guns and roses. Let us take control of the situation again, together.

I am tempted to come up with another version of Guns and Roses, something that will encourage my government and its leadership to find solutions to restore the black dignity. Let us not become the victims of our own history. I wish we could unite against being divided; don't we belong to the same political party, haven't we fought against the apartheid regime together, haven't we fought for equal rights for all? If I were as gifted as Lucky was, I'd have the courage and guts to compose this song.

These guns and roses of our time,

brother fighting brother!

What are we fighting for?

Is it who is able to lay their hands first on

the millions of the nation?

Who can steal smart, who can drive the top

of-the-range imported cars?

These guns and roses of my time, are all

about amassing wealth from a system that

you're supposed to protect!

I love you my brother, let us fight for the

emancipation of our people.

But when it comes to this money thing, we are

not brothers, we are not comrades, these are

the guns and roses of my time.

I miss Lucky so much; these are the things we would have debated over time. I look at the political side of things and assume that there is no one to share my views with, in case I offend people. And I know I will; people are comfortable belonging with the masses. I would rather take the road less travelled, knowing that no one determines the safety of my journey, except myself. The majority take sides, not bothering about how messed up the side is – as long as it is the side of the elites or the most popular camp or what benefits them. I was trained in the highest university, which boasts the likes of Bishop Tutu, Frank Chikane, Rev. Maja, Rev.

Ndanganeni Phaswana, Rev. Chere, the Dean Mminele and many other great men and women who had the same spirit of discernment as Lucky Dube. Their source is one; they looked at what the Bible said about it, and when they preached it, Lucky sang it.

The class of the South African Council of Churches is a class I am very proud to associate with. It is the class of order, honour and character. I hear that the Bible does not work in politics but there are politics in the Bible. The class of the SACC played a critical role in the fight against apartheid, but I am sure they are in the same position I am in today, a position that says this is not what we were fighting for. We were fighting for true liberation of black people; we were not fighting for half a liberation. If we'd known at that time that we would be given programmes that were not designed for black people, supposedly in the name of empowering blacks economically, I don't think we'd have wasted our time sacrificing the way we did for political activists, for this nyakafater. We didn't work for our liberation to be an enemy with itself, for brothers to be fighting with each other. Of this I am sure. If you ask me whether Lucky would have sung a different song today, I would say no. Until real transformation of the rights of South Africans favours the majority who live in this country as their birthright, I wouldn't hold my breath. Our struggle is far from over. Some of our own brothers whom we depended on have turned their backs on the struggle just because they are

financially comfortable. They have forgotten that, at some point, they themselves were preaching about the sharing of wealth. Who are they sharing their wealth with today? This is not orderly; the struggle is not yet over, my brothers. You'll have to come back to your senses and think again.

Lucky's home was in Newcastle, Kwa-Zulu Natal. He had to drive more than 300 km to Johannesburg to his office. For twenty plus years he did this trip over and over again. The trip took him through the beautiful Midlands – rolling farm countryside that must have reminded him of his childhood. I think the experience was painful.

Let me say that he re-lived his childhood until the day he died – he couldn't run away from it. He never forgot where he came from; seeing the farmworkers' children walking long distances and asking for lifts from strangers each time he drove past affected him greatly. He knew how it felt to walk the distance on an empty stomach and wished he could do something for these children. So that's why I wouldn't hold my breath about him singing a different tune today, when there's still so much suffering around us. What are we going to do about it? We should be at the forefront of running our country, because we are its eyes and ears. You may remember the scandal in which the government gave millions of Rands to a church minister who turned out to be a conman. The funds were for a school that never materialised. This happened right under the nose of government in the Ekurhuleni municipality area; all because the neighbouring community was not interested enough in what was going on in that area, or they were just too complacent to do anything. We are all responsible for our country and its interests are ours; its business is ours. The time for blaming one another is over. We need order in this, our times of guns and roses.

5. A TRUE AFRICAN HERO

Lucky's music carried a very strong message. Underlying his compositions there was always a realistic and practical message;he just wanted to tell it like it is. Perhaps not with the intention of deliberately upsetting and irritating others, but to bring to the attention of those on the other side of the fence that people are aware of what is going on and they are not stupid. Not many people are brave enough to tell the bald truth and nothing but the truth,without fearing rejection, or worse.

His music speaks for those who are voiceless all over the world; he was an ambassador of love and peace with his music, which impacted on many souls globally. When the world needed peace and healing, Lucky Dube would be called to calm the people down. I'm talking about an impact that African leaders were aware of, and have known, but never acknowledged to the man himself. They knew when they needed him, the restorer of peace and order.

After the genocide in Rwanda, in 1994, he was asked to come and calm down the nation that was divided. According to the Rwandans, he was the only one who could soothe the pain of the nation, the only one who could bring the two fighting groups together in one stadium, for which the outcome would be peaceful.

It was a moving experience for Lucky. Experiencing such after the war was something that would stay in his heart for a very long time; it tore at his heart to learn that the fighting was orchestrated by some idiots whom I have not time to mention. Again in 2006, after they had their elections, he was called to ease the tensions. For some odd reason it seems politicians will always know who to use in situations like these; they understand what music does to people. In this instance they knew what Lucky's music would do to the Rwandans. I am deeply interested in knowing what effect Lucky's music has on emotions. I know what it does to me, personally, but it would be interesting to know how deep it goes for the rest of the world. I am saying this because I have watched, with interest, the followers of his music. I have also tried to profile the followers of his music; I am puzzled by this. He was taken through the memorial where the history of the genocide was written. I was a part of this journey with him. I know how I felt then; I know how I still feel today. I won't waste my time talking about it either – it breaks my heart. Each piece of history will be conserved for many generations to come so that this sort of thing won't be repeated ever again.

Lucky was regarded as a peacemaker; people believed that if he addressed nations, there would be calmness. In his song, It's a Crazy World, he warns of world wars being instigated by the leaders themselves. When they don't agree with each other they divide the nations and fuel fights which end up in serious wars. The Rwandan genocide was a good example of this, and even though he wrote this song long before the genocide, he had a gift of prophecy. He saw the things that none of us see; he penned them, rehearsed them into rhythms and melodies, and those that had ears for his music heard and sang along. Those who could dance to his rhythm moved and danced to it.

At the time of writing this book, I wasn't sure whether to term it a cat fight or a powerstruggle in the leadership of our ruling party. Our former president, Thabo Mbeki, was threatening to release to the nation information relating to a part of our history that we do not know, information he was prepared to share. Perhaps what he is referring to is the very thing that we need as a people. He agrees that the people have not always been told the truth and that what he is about to unleash is a piece of the missing jigsaw puzzle.

I quote: "I have various facts at my disposal which have not as yet seen the light of day, but which are essential pieces of the jigsaw puzzle which explains the evolution of South Africa over a number of decades, to this day". This, after the Special Investigations Unit head, Willem Heath, accused him of orchestrating and initiating the rape and corruption charges against current president Zuma. He admitted that Heath had opened a Pandora's box. I say the idea is too scary so please don't open it, lest some bones fall out of it – bones that could destroy our nation. At his level of maturity, and being former president, I would have thought that he would let sleeping dogs lie. I hadn't expected such a statement from a former statesman; I feel that no matter what, there are things the nation should be protected from. I do not blame him though, he is only human, he chooses when to be humane, now he is playing Mr nice guy. Perhaps he cant deal with the humiliation of his recalling. To think that Lucky Dube was an ambassador for South Africa who had to protect him during his highly criticized opinion on the HIV does not necessarily cause AIDS and that ARVs are toxic. Lucky went through a lot during that time, people forgot he was an artist promoting his own music, he was regarded as someone who would shed more light on political issues as well. And because Lucky's music dwells on the suffering and the plight of the poor, this question from the media could not have been avoided, the people needed answers from him. Lucky could not have advised people to take ARVs, nor could he have advised them not to take them. He worked around a solution and applied an African principle of culture and sharing information so that people could understand the challenge of AIDS facing Africa. He understood Mbeki's opinion and how his view was manipulated as it threatened a certain agenda. At the time Mbeki said this, people hadn't been equipped with information on the AIDS virus, how to deal with it and with each other because if we knew then we wouldn't have lost so many of our brothers and sisters. Sometimes dealing with our own problems as Africans is better than if we allowed others to tell us how we should handle our own issues. Lucky had known of the Ugandan strategy of fighting the pandemic, it was purely African and it was a great success. A decision made by Africans for the Africans. We should as Africans listen to each other, without influences of any sort, we can debate and argue on issues that affect us. You can take the best antiretrovirals in the world, if you take them on a poor diet, they remain toxic, any medication however good, is prescribed, if it has to be taken after food, there is a reason for that. If you give poor people antiretrovirals even if you gave them proper information, they will die in their numbers. What is key here is how they should take the medication, and what good would government be doing if it bought ARVs and supplied them to people who had no food in their homes. A caring government would not be spending millions on medications that would end up killing its own faster than the virus itself. Mbeki's viewpoint was right, we could have silently dealt with our AIDS problem the African way. There are certain things you do that you don't shout out to the world to hear, this is when we rely on our cultures for solutions. This is a lesson we have learned, we should discern as a people. If it hadn't been for Lucky I would also still be holding Mbeki's viewpoint as an embarrassment for South Africa, Lucky made me understand that which I could not grasp. Sometimes leaders also need to understand that there are certain social messages that are better conveyed by other people on their behalf. Instead of being hated and sidelined, he should have been used as a blind spot, he was one, he knew these things before they could manifest themselves into problems for he lived with real people in real times. Take note. I also wish our government could understand that when we are out there, we defend our own, sometimes we find ourselves in nasty situations where we are called names by others because we are on the side of government, Lucky suffered this a lot, some thought he was not radical enough to be a rastaman. You risk rejection from your own if you stand for the truth it doesn't matter who's side you are on or how right you are. Lucky took a show in Namibia the one time, only to find that it was the oppressor's show. He was never forgiven for taking that show. Those that are in showbiz understand and will attest to the fact that when we accept invitations, I mean us managers, we ask a few almost intelligent questions, we are interested in the capacity of the venue, where the venue is, is it government or a private show, indoor or outdoor, we don't ask if it is for the Democratic Party or the Labour Party. We decide the artists don't, it is our business to find work for the artist, they don't prescribe to us if we should take male only shows or blacks only shows. The artist only gets there and finds that it is what it is, they do the work they are contracted to do and get their smart selves out of there. The next time anyone points a finger at an artist for anything, they should think twice! For Lucky the South African struggle was his own struggle but he wasn't going to be quiet about issues that affect humanity, the abuses of power, the crimes committed by those that are in power, the corruption and the many ills committed by government. Peace loving artists don't sing about issues to gain popularity, they sing about issues because singing is a way and means of sending messages, the message gets there quicker, not distorted and can be heard anytime and joyfully. It is for our benefit to have these artists, honestly it is for our own good, they are societies blind spots, we should embrace them. Most of them do not possess qualifications from prestigious Universities they touch many lives in ways that we can never understand. When Lucky fell, our own government failed to elevate his status in fact I suspect the then President must have celebrated. When the whole world accorded Lucky the honour that he so richly deserved, the man just decided he was making one speech he did it because it was expected. I doubt if he meant anything he said in his speech which when I look at it today, sounds incomplete or am I delusional.

President Thabo Mbeki extends Condolences to Lucky Dube's Family

Pretoria - President Thabo Mbeki today, Friday, 19 October extended South Africa's heartfelt condolences to the family of Luck Dube, the South African musician who was killed on Thursday 18 October 2007 in Johannesburg.

Speaking moments before his departure to Paris, France, President Mbeki said "It is a sad moment because late last night, I was told that Lucky Dube had been killed, apparently in an attempted hijacking in Johannesburg. It is indeed very sad that this happened to an outstanding South African, outstanding musician, world renowned. I would really like to convey our condolences to his family, to all music lovers in our country and the rest of the world and to all our people.

"Because even as we prepare to celebrate the victory of the Springboks, we must also, grief the death of this outstanding South African, and indeed make a commitment that we shall continue to act together as a people, to confront this terrible scourge, the scourge of crime, which has taken the lives of too many of our people and does so, everyday" continued President Mbeki.

Perhaps, when we bring back the cup that will also be a salute to a fellow artist, as Springboks are artists, a fellow artist to the life of a great and really great South African artist Lucky Dube" concluded President Mbeki

Issued by the Presidency
Union Buildings
Pretoria
0001
19 October 2007

I must admit, former President Mbeki's speech must have been misplaced somewhere, I doubt if a statesman could deliver such an empty speech. I know the writings of Mbeki and this could not have been him and this is my personal opinion. This could not have been the man I grew to know to seize every opportunity he had to drive home most of his political agendas, an intellectual giant, smart and smooth. The man many of us admired and pinned our hopes on for the future of our children and their children's children. This couldn't have been the man whom Lucky Dube defended in the renowned world he mentions Lucky was known. This is not the type of speech for a world renowned artist, no I don't think so. I am sure all South Africans have forgotten what he said that day, there was nothing to remember about what he said that day, maybe the Springboks will remember because this happened during their participation in the world cup in 2007 which they won that year. But other than that, nothing memorable. And I am sure he knew no one would make follow up on whether he kept his promise of celebrating the artist when the Springboks won, let alone showing up or sending a personal message. When South Africa mourned

Lucky, the statesman was on his way to Soweto that afternoon to honor one of our great artists, sis Busi Mhlongo who succumbed to cancer in June of 2010. May sis Busi's soul rest in perfect peace, she was an inspiration to many of us. I am not sure why I am mentioning this about Mbeki, but I can't just help myself perhaps Lucky's spirit is haunting me! Well done to the former statesman, the people have noted that! When one of our legends Mahlathini died, my then President Thabo Mbeki seized the moment, I read all the messages that we received from all over the world. There was a lot of ululation as I read each letter from people expressing their admiration for our legend who had died a pauper. Most of these letters were from the International community. I remember how the music industry embraced our then President, he had attended the funeral amidst his busy schedule, the sort of support our industry needed and still need to this day. I remember I was the last person before former President Mbeki took on stage. A proud moment for me. The sound that was used for the funeral service was that of Lucky Dube, we had requested him to assist us free of charge so we could give Mahlathini a decent send off . Lucky Dube had a show that day and had to rush to his show immediately after the funeral service, but he went out of his way to honor another fallen musician. Our former President spoke from the microphone of Lucky Dube, an act Lucky Dube himself embraced, former President Mbeki represented hope for us. There is one thing about Lucky Dube that made him the person he was, he was a true African hero, over his 25-year career it was not only his lyrics that spoke of pain and suffering."The melody comes with some sorrow," Ghanaian musician Batman Samini explains. "It tells exactly where he's crying from. The right melody is carrying the right message to you. Most Ghanaians could tell South Africa's grief through Lucky's cry." Batman told the BBC.

Whether the former president was aware of Lucky's involvement or not, Lucky Dube was a peace maker a peacemaker who represented his own government in the continent, when there was a war elsewhere the African people would ask for Lucky Dube's

109

intervention. He stepped out and represented the country and the then president with his voice, a rare balance for a talent to come out of a Country and represent his own with his own talent. "It takes me back to the early stage of the Liberian civil crisis when we were looking for food and shelter - for somebody to give us back hope. It was the voice of Lucky Dube that brought hope to many Liberians," Liberian fan Tom Takor told the BBC on hearing about Dube's death. Lucky went deep where nobody dared to tread, he smelt burning flesh, he saw the last flames of war torn countries, on our behalf. He came amongst us. We cannot claim to not have known, I know for sure that the then president was aware of Lucky's involvement in the activities of peace interventions, our foreign missions do report these activities. Some of these activities are referred to us by the foreign missions. I facilitated Lucky's involvement for Liberia when all else failed to restore peace in Liberia, the Red Cross requested Lucky to intervene and restore their peace. Lucky's status did not have to be elevated during his demise, no don't get me wrong. All that needed to happen was to acknowledge his work, as a nation, one of our giants had fallen, we were a mourning nation. What hurts the world the most is that it seems we do not care and they will keep wondering why this is so. To this day Lucky's band is still touring the world, people believe they still need to connect with his spirit for peace sake. We are required to answer hurtful questions about why the South African government did not have a presence at Lucky's funeral when the world was in solidarity with us. We cannot answer those questions, perhaps we need to ask this question ourselves and find the answers, can anyone help? Looking back the only presence we had was that of the Arts and Culture Ministry, Professor Keorapetse Kgosietsile who read a letter from the then Minister of Arts and Culture Pallo Jordan because the Minister could not make it to the memorial. It is the same world who believes that there is still unfinished business pertaining to Lucky's legacy. We are not having fun having to answer these questions, it is heavy on us, and it seems the question will not go away anytime soon. This is how Lucky was and still is revered in the rest of the world. As the then CEO of the SABC Dali

Mpofu indicated in his speech "Lucky Dube is still communicating with us, even in his death. The question is whether we are listening to his message. I think he is asking what has gone wrong with us". Forgive me former President, I am getting personal with you, Lucky Dube was my friend, he was my mentor, he gave my people hope, I still have to answer questions asked by the many loyal fans. Why? Luckily I have not been in an accident, I have not been shot at, I've avoided driving since Lucky died for fear of being killed for a piece of steel, or being mistaken for a foreigner as if foreigners are less than human and deserve to be killed. I live a life of terror in my own country, fearing that I would be killed for what I believe in, many have been. I am thankful that I am still alive and need to tell this story as quickly as possible in case I am mistaken for a foreigner. This story to me is humbling to humanity, it is a story that makes my heart beat, I am a proud African before I am a South African, black, female, a single mother and I am proud of it. You made me conscious of who I was at some point and I have been proud for being who I am since because you gave me the assurance that I am an African. In case you do not know who I am, this is who I am. *I am the grandchild who tip toes to lay fresh flowers on the Boer commercial fields of Skeerpoort when the Boers are not watching. Laying these flowers in the hope that my grandfather's spirit will still pick my troubled voice out of the soil and grains and plants as I cry out to him in chants of his father's name and clan name, for his grave was levelled to make space for the hectares upon hectares of commercial fields that have to feed my people. I am the grandchild whose grandmother's grave is the property of the Boer nestled in the Magalies mountain.* Let me borrow from a statement you made on the occasion of the adoption by the Constitutional Assembly of The Republic of South Africa Constitution Bill 1996, 8 May on behalf of the ANC.

I am an African....

Chairperson, Esteemed President of the democratic Republic, Honourable Members of the Constitutional Assembly, Our distinguished domestic and foreign guests, Friends,

On an occasion such as this, we should, perhaps, start from the beginning.

So, let me begin.

I am an African.

I owe my being to the hills and the valleys, the mountains and the glades, the rivers, the deserts, the trees, the flowers, the seas and the ever-changing seasons that define the face of our native land.

My body has frozen in our frosts and in our latter day snows. It has thawed in the warmth of our sunshine and melted in the heat of the midday sun. The crack and the rumble of the summer thunders, lashed by startling lightning, have been a cause both of trembling and of hope.

The fragrances of nature have been as pleasant to us as the sight of the wild blooms of the citizens of the veld.

The dramatic shapes of the Drakensberg, the soil-coloured waters of the Lekoa, iGqili noThukela, and the sands of the Kgalagadi, have all been panels of the set on the natural stage on which we act out the foolish deeds of the theatre of our day.

At times, and in fear, I have wondered whether I should concede equal citizenship of our country to the leopard and the lion, the elephant and the springbok, the hyena, the black mamba and the pestilential mosquito.

A human presence among all these, a feature on the face of our native land thus defined, I know that none dare challenge me when I say - I am an African!

I owe my being to the Khoi and the San whose desolate souls haunt the great expanses of the beautiful Cape - they who fell victim to the most merciless genocide our native land has ever seen, they who were the first to lose their lives in the struggle to defend our

112

freedom and independence and they who, as a people, perished in the result.

Today, as a country, we keep an audible silence about these ancestors of the generations that live, fearful to admit the horror of a former deed, seeking to obliterate from our memories a cruel occurrence which, in its remembering, should teach us not and never to be inhuman again.

I am formed of the migrants who left Europe to find a new home on our native land. Whatever their own actions, they remain still, part of me.

In my veins courses the blood of the Malay slaves who came from the East. Their proud dignity informs my bearing, their culture a part of my essence. The stripes they bore on their bodies from the lash of the slave master are a reminder embossed on my consciousness of what should not be done.

I am the grandchild of the warrior men and women that Hintsa and Sekhukhune led, the patriots that Cetshwayo and Mphephu took to battle, the soldiers Moshoeshoe and Ngungunyane taught never to dishonour the cause of freedom.

My mind and my knowledge of myself is formed by the victories that are the jewels in our African crown, the victories we earned from Isandhlwana to Khartoum, as Ethiopians and as the Ashanti of Ghana, as the Berbers of the desert.

I am the grandchild who lays fresh flowers on the Boer graves at St Helena and the Bahamas, who sees in the mind's eye and suffers the suffering of a simple peasant folk, death, concentration camps, destroyed homesteads, a dream in ruins.

I am the child of Nongqause. I am he who made it possible to trade in the world markets in diamonds, in gold, in the same food for which my stomach yearns.

I come of those who were transported from India and China, whose being resided in the fact, solely, that they were able to provide physical labour, who taught me that we could both be at home and be foreign, who taught me that human existence itself demanded that freedom was a necessary condition for that human existence.

Being part of all these people, and in the knowledge that none dare contest that assertion, I shall claim that - I am an African.

I have seen our country torn asunder as these, all of whom are my people, engaged one another in a titanic battle, the one redress a wrong that had been caused by one to another and the other, to defend the indefensible.

I have seen what happens when one person has superiority of force over another, when the stronger appropriate to themselves the prerogative even to annul the injunction that God created all men and women in His image.

I know what it signifies when race and colour are used to determine who is human and who, sub-human.

I have seen the destruction of all sense of self-esteem, the consequent striving to be what one is not, simply to acquire some of the benefits which those who had improved themselves as masters had ensured that they enjoy.

I have experience of the situation in which race and colour is used to enrich some and impoverish the rest.

I have seen the corruption of minds and souls as (word not readable) of the pursuit of an ignoble effort to perpetrate a veritable crime against humanity.

I have seen concrete expression of the denial of the dignity of a human being emanating from the conscious, systemic and systematic oppressive and repressive activities of other human beings.

114

There the victims parade with no mask to hide the brutish reality - the beggars, the prostitutes, the street children, those who seek solace in substance abuse, those who have to steal to assuage hunger, those who have to lose their sanity because to be sane is to invite pain.

Perhaps the worst among these, who are my people, are those who have learnt to kill for a wage. To these the extent of death is directly proportional to their personal welfare.

And so, like pawns in the service of demented souls, they kill in furtherance of the political violence in KwaZulu-Natal. They murder the innocent in the taxi wars.

They kill slowly or quickly in order to make profits from the illegal trade in narcotics. They are available for hire when husband wants to murder wife and wife, husband.

Among us prowl the products of our immoral and amoral past - killers who have no sense of the worth of human life, rapists who have absolute disdain for the women of our country, animals who would seek to benefit from the vulnerability of the children, the disabled and the old, the rapacious who brook no obstacle in their quest for self-enrichment.

All this I know and know to be true because I am an African!

Because of that, I am also able to state this fundamental truth that I am born of a people who are heroes and heroines.

I am born of a people who would not tolerate oppression.

I am of a nation that would not allow that fear of death, torture, imprisonment, exile or persecution should result in the perpetuation of injustice.

The great masses who are our mother and father will not permit that the behaviour of the few results in the description of our

115

country and people as barbaric.

Patient because history is on their side, these masses do not despair because today the weather is bad. Nor do they turn triumphalist when, tomorrow, the sun shines.

Whatever the circumstances they have lived through and because of that experience, they are determined to define for themselves who they are and who they should be.

We are assembled here today to mark their victory in acquiring and exercising their right to formulate their own definition of what it means to be African.

The Constitution whose adoption we celebrate constitutes an unequivocal statement that we refuse to accept that our Africanness shall be defined by our race, colour, gender or historical origins.

It is a firm assertion made by ourselves that South Africa belongs to all who live in it, Black and White.

It gives concrete expression to the sentiment we share as Africans, and will defend to the death, that the people shall govern.

It recognises the fact that the dignity of the individual is both an objective which society must pursue, and is a goal which cannot be separated from the material well-being of that individual.

It seeks to create the situation in which all our people shall be free from fear, including the fear of the oppression of one national group by another, the fear of the disempowerment of one social echelon by another, the fear of the use of state power to deny anybody their fundamental human rights and the fear of tyranny.

It aims to open the doors so that those who were disadvantaged can assume their place in society as equals with their fellow human beings without regard to colour, race, gender, age or geographic dispersal.

It provides the opportunity to enable each one and all to state their views, promote them, strive for their implementation in the process of governance without fear that a contrary view will be met with repression.

It creates a law-governed society which shall be inimical to arbitrary rule.

It enables the resolution of conflicts by peaceful means rather than resort to force.

It rejoices in the diversity of our people and creates the space for all of us voluntarily to define ourselves as one people.

As an African, this is an achievement of which I am proud, proud without reservation and proud without any feeling of conceit.

Our sense of elevation at this moment also derives from the fact that this magnificent product is the unique creation of African hands and African minds.

But it also constitutes a tribute to our loss of vanity that we could, despite the temptation to treat ourselves as an exceptional fragment of humanity, draw on the accumulated experience and wisdom of all humankind, to define for ourselves what we want to be.

Together with the best in the world, we too are prone to pettiness, petulance, selfishness and short-sightedness.

But it seems to have happened that we looked at ourselves and said the time had come that we make a super-human effort to be other than human, to respond to the call to create for ourselves a glorious future, to remind ourselves of the Latin saying: Gloria est consequenda - Glory must be sought after!

Today it feels good to be an African.

It feels good that I can stand here as a South African and as a foot

117

soldier of a titanic African army, the African National Congress, to say to all the parties represented here, to the millions who made an input into the processes we are concluding, to our outstanding compatriots who have presided over the birth of our founding document, to the negotiators who pitted their wits one against the other, to the unseen stars who shone unseen as the management and administration of the Constitutional Assembly, the advisers, experts and publicists, to the mass communication media, to our friends across the globe - congratulations and well done!

I am an African.

I am born of the peoples of the continent of Africa.

The pain of the violent conflict that the peoples of Liberia, Somalia, the Sudan, Burundi and Algeria is a pain I also bear.

The dismal shame of poverty, suffering and human degradation of my continent is a blight that we share.

The blight on our happiness that derives from this and from our drift to the periphery of the ordering of human affairs leaves us in a persistent shadow of despair.

This is a savage road to which nobody should be condemned.

This thing that we have done today, in this small corner of a great continent that has contributed so decisively to the evolution of humanity says that Africa reaffirms that she is continuing her rise from the ashes.

Whatever the setbacks of the moment, nothing can stop us now! Whatever the difficulties, Africa shall be at peace! However improbable it may sound to the sceptics, Africa will prosper!

Whoever we may be, whatever our immediate interest, however much we carry baggage from our past, however much we have been caught by the fashion of cynicism and loss of faith in the capacity of the people, let us err today and say - nothing can stop us now!

Thank you.

I promised to give a standing ovation to this courageous speech, but before I do I thought let me pause for a while and reflect on the great speech. I paused and I paused, I am still pausing as I got infuriated by your own admission

"I have seen our country torn asunder as these, all of whom are my people, engaged one another in a titanic battle, the one redress a wrong that had been caused by one to another and the other, to defend the indefensible.

I have seen what happens when one person has superiority of force over another, when the stronger appropriate to themselves the prerogative even to annul the injunction that God created all men and women in His image".

I reflected on this, they say history repeats itself, it is true, when you are power drunk, you lose sight of many things, you miss even the obvious. The great speech was what made us South Africans admire our then leader, we had fallen in love with his mind, he had won our hearts, we were proud of him, we had a great leader amongst our own. He worked smart as a leader, the quality of his character was admirable, I give him that, he had his own faults, we all do. Today I sing a different tune, former President Mbeki you have torn the South African nation asunder, all of whom you referred to as your people. Your superiority complex as a statesman is the reason our country is torn asunder today. It is amazing you were able to identify the superiority of a force over another but you could not help yourself to apply same when you were given power. South Africa's problems today are the result of your superiority ego yesterday. The great speech that we have learned to associate and remind ourselves to be proud as Africans has amounted to nothing but words with no meaning. I do not want to associate with it as it means nothing, what glory shall we seek after you delivered us from a promise to shambles the nation is facing today, as you can see your speech has made it into my book not as a source of inspiration it should have been but as an ego of a man we entrusted a future of a glorious nation. I can unpack every word of every sentence you wrote and humbly send it so you can remind yourself, that you were once a proud African! We ate from the palms of your hands, we fed like little hungry children, some suckled from the wisdom your speech represented only to realise it was all air we fed on. Who is African, I cannot hide the resentment I've harboured for as long as Lucky passed on through a crime that threatened to dwarf his legacy. It is the world that continues to elevate the stature of our legend, it is the very world that we agree with that Lucky was not accorded the honour that he so deserved. We shall not lose hope, we remain African for we will learn from intellectual giants that left great legacies for us and our children, we shall know through these who we are. We were supposed to learn great things from you, not democracy today and a country in shambles tomorrow. A great sacrifice will have to go into the reclaiming of our dignity in the near future, for now, we are in shambles and I still maintain you delivered us into shambles. You failed to set the proper tone of our leadership, exposing the glorious nation to situations that have dented our democracy.

 I borrow from one of Africa's greats, Pixley Ka Isaka Seme, this is a great inspiration for me because I remain an African.

The Regeneration of Africa by Pixley Ka Isaka Seme

5 April 1906

I have chosen to speak to you on this occasion upon "The Regeneration of Africa."

I am an African, and I set my pride in my race over against a hostile public opinion. Men have tried to compare races on the basis of some equality. In all the works of nature, equality, if by it we mean identity, is an impossible dream! Search the universe! You will find no two units alike. The scientists tell us there are no two cells, no two atoms, identical.

Nature has bestowed upon each a peculiar individuality, an exclusive patent from the great giants of the forest to the tenderest blade. Catch in your hand, if you please, the gentle flakes of snow. Each is a perfect gem, a new creation; it shines in its own glory – a work of art different from all of its aerial companions.

Man, the crowning achievement of nature, defies analysis. He is a mystery through all ages and for all time. The races of mankind are composed of free and unique individuals. An attempt to compare them on the basis of equality can never be finally satisfactory. Each is self.

My thesis stands on this truth; time has proved it. In all races, genius is like a spark, which, concealed in the bosom of a flint, bursts forth at the summoning stroke. It may arise anywhere and in any race.

I would ask you not to compare Africa to Europe or to any other continent. I make this request not from any fear that such comparison might bring humiliation upon Africa. The reason I have stated,-a common standard is impossible!

Come with me to the ancient capital of Egypt, Thebes, the city of one hundred gates. The grandeur of its venerable ruins and the gigantic proportions of its architecture reduce to insignificance the boasted monuments of other nations.

The pyramids of Egypt are structures to which the world presents nothing comparable. The mighty monuments seem to look with disdain on every other work of human art and to vie with nature herself. All the glory of Egypt belongs to Africa and her people. These monuments are the indestructible memorials of their great and original genius. it is not through Egypt alone that Africa claims such unrivalled historic

gleam, Where is it now, the glory and the dream?"

Oh, for that historian who, with the open pen of truth, will bring to Africa's claim the strength of written proof. He will tell of a race whose onward tide was often swelled with tears achievements.

I could have spoken of the pyramids of Ethiopia, which, though inferior in size to those of Egypt, far surpass them in architectural beauty; their sepulchres which evince the highest purity of taste, and of many prehistoric ruins in other parts of Africa.

In such ruins Africa is like the golden sun, that, having sunk beneath the western horizon, still plays upon the world which he sustained and enlightened in his career.

Justly the world now demands-

"Whither is fled the visionary, but in whose heart bondage has not quenched the fire of former years. He will write that in these later days when Earth's noble ones are named, she has a roll of honor too, of whom she is not ashamed.

The giant is awakening!

From the four corners of the earth Africa's sons, who have been proved through fire and sword, are marching to the future's golden door bearing the records of deeds of valor done.

Mr. Calhoun, I believe, was the most philosophical of all the slaveholders. He said once that if he could find a black man who could understand the Greek syntax, he would then consider their race human, and his attitude toward enslaving them would therefore change.

What might have been the sensation kindled by the Greek syntax in the mind of the famous Southerner, I have so far been unable to discover; but oh, I envy the moment that was lost! And woe to the tongues that refused to tell the truth!

If any such were among the now living, I could show him among black men of pure African blood those who could repeat the Koran from memory, skilled in Latin, Greek and Hebrew, Arabic and Chaldaic – men great in wisdom and profound knowledge – one professor of philosophy in a celebrated German university; one corresponding member of the French Academy of Sciences, who regularly transmitted to that society meteorological observations, and hydrographical journals and papers on botany and geology; another whom many ages call "The Wise," whose authority Mahomet himself frequently appealed to in the Koran in support of his own opinion-men of wealth and active benevolence, those whose distinguished talents and reputation have made them famous in the cabinet and in the field, officers of artillery in the great armies of Europe, generals and lieutenant generals in the armies of Peter the Great in Russia and Napoleon in France, presidents of free republics, kings of independent nations which have burst their way to liberty by their own vigor.

There are many other Africans who have shown marks of genius and high character sufficient to redeem their race from the charges which I am now considering.

Ladies and gentlemen, the day of great exploring expeditions in Africa is over!

Man knows his home now in a sense never known before. Many great and holy men have evinced a passion for the day you are now witnessing their prophetic vision shot through many unborn centuries to this very hour.

"Men shall run to and fro," said Daniel, "and knowledge shall increase upon the earth."

Oh, how true! See the triumph of human genius to-day!

Science has searched out the deep things of nature, surprised the secrets of the most distant stars, disentombed the memorials of everlasting hills, taught the lightning to speak, the vapors to toil and the winds to worship-spanned the sweeping rivers, tunneled the longest mountain range-made the world a vast whispering gallery, and has brought foreign nations into one civilized family.

This all-powerful contact says even to the most backward race, you cannot remain where you are, you cannot fall back, you must advance!

A great century has come upon us. No race possessing the inherent capacity to survive can resist and remain unaffected by this influence of contact and intercourse, the backward with the advanced. This influence constitutes the very essence of efficient progress and of civilization.

From these heights of the twentieth century I again ask you to cast your eyes south of the Desert of Sahara. If you could go with me to the oppressed Congos and ask, What does it mean, that now, for liberty, they fight like men and die like martyrs; if you would go with me to Bechuanaland, face their council of headmen and ask what motives caused them recently to decree so emphatically that alcoholic drinks shall not enter their country – visit their king, Khama, ask for what cause he leaves the gold and ivory palace of his ancestors, its mountain strongholds and all its august ceremony, to wander daily from village to village through all his kingdom, without a guard or any decoration of his rank – a preacher of industry and education, and an apostle of the new order of things; if you would ask Menelik what means this that Abyssinia is now looking across the ocean – oh, if you could read the letters that come to us from Zululand – you too would be convinced that the elevation of the African race is evidently a part of the new order of things that belong to this new and powerful period.

The African already recognizes his anomalous position and desires a change. The brighter day is rising upon Africa. Already I seem to

124

see her chains dissolved, her desert plains red with harvest, her Abyssinia and her Zululand the seats of science and religion, reflecting the glory of the rising sun from the spires of their churches and universities.

Her Congo and her Gambia whitened with commerce, her crowded cities sending forth the hum of business, and all her sons employed in advancing the victories of peace-greater and more abiding than the spoils of war.

Yes, the regeneration of Africa belongs to this new and powerful period!

By this term regeneration I wish to be understood to mean the entrance into a new life, embracing the diverse phases of a higher, complex existence. The basic factor which assures their regeneration resides in the awakened race-consciousness. This gives them a clear perception of their elemental needs and of their undeveloped powers. It therefore must lead them to the attainment of that higher and advanced standard of life.

The African people, although not a strictly homogeneous race, possess a common fundamental sentiment which is everywhere manifest, crystallizing itself into one common controlling idea. Conflicts and strife are rapidly disappearing before the fusing force of this enlightened perception of the true intertribal relation, which relation should subsist among a people with a common destiny. Agencies of a social, economic and religious advance tell of a new spirit which, acting as a leavening ferment, shall raise the anxious and aspiring mass to the level of their ancient glory.

The ancestral greatness, the unimpaired genius, and the recuperative power of the race, its irrepressibility, which assures its permanence, constitute the African's greatest source of inspiration. He has refused to camp forever on the borders of the industrial world; having learned that knowledge is power, he is educating his children.

You find them in Edinburgh, in Cambridge, and in the great schools of Germany. These return to their country like arrows, to drive darkness from the land. I hold that his industrial and educational initiative, and his untiring devotion to these activities, must be regarded as positive evidences of this process of his regeneration.

The regeneration of Africa means that a new and unique civilization is soon to be added to the world. The African is not a proletarian in the world of science and art. He has precious creations of his own, of ivory, of copper and of gold, fine, plated willow-ware and weapons of superior workmanship.

Civilization resembles an organic being in its development-it is born, it perishes, and it can propagate itself. More particularly, it resembles a plant, it takes root in the teeming earth, and when the seeds fall in other soils new varieties sprout up. The most essential departure of this new civilization is that it shall be thoroughly spiritual and humanistic -indeed a regeneration moral and eternal!

O Africa!

Like some great century plant that shall bloom

In ages hence, we watch thee; in our dream

See in thy swamps the Prospero of our stream;

Thy doors unlocked, where knowledge in her tomb Hath lain innumerable years in gloom.

Then shalt thou, walking with that morning gleam,

Shine as thy sister lands with equal beam.

A brief overview of Isaka ka Seme;

He was born in Daggakraal, then in the Colony of Natal, at the Inanda mission station of the American Zulu Mission of

the American Board of Commissioners for Foreign Missions. He
graduated from Mount Hermon School, MA, in 1902 (now the
Northfield Mount Hermon School). He attended Adams
College which was part of the mission.

His mother was a sister of John Langalibalele Dube, and descended
from a local chief. At 17 years of age Seme left to study in the U.S.,
first at the Mount Hermon School and then Columbia University. In
1906, his senior year at University, he was awarded the Curtis
Medal, Columbia's highest oratorical honor. He subsequently
decided to become an attorney. In October 1906 he was admitted
to Oxford University to read for the degree of Bachelor of Civil
Law; while at Oxford he was a member of Jesus College.

Seme returned to South Africa in 1911. In response to the formation
of the Union of South Africa, he worked with several other young
African leaders recently returned from university studies in
England, Richard Msimang, George Montsioa andAlfred Mangena,
and with established leaders of the South African Native
Convention in Johannesburg to promote the formation of a national
organization that would unify various African groups from the
former separate colonies, now provinces. In January 1912 these
efforts bore fruit with the founding meeting of the South African
Native National Congress, later renamed the African National
Congress (Walshe 1970, Odendaal 1984). Seme was also the lawyer
of Queen RegentLabotsibeni of Swaziland, through who the first
ANC newspaper Abantu-Batho was financed. Later on in 1922
Seme accompanied King Sobhuza II as part of a delegation to
london to meet British authorities and the King regarding the land
proclamation in Swaziland.

Seme's nationalist organizing among Africans paralleled the
contemporaneous efforts of Mohandas Gandhi with South African
Indians.

Seme was very close to the Zulu and Swazi royal families. This is
primarily symbolized by his marriage to Phikisele Harriet Dinizulu

the daughter of Zulu king Dinuzulu and to Lozinja daughter of Swazi King Mbandzeni.

I would have been a proud African woman to read your biography to my children and their children's children in the years of my old age. I would have read your story not as a destructors story of our lives, but as a story of hope of our lives.

You were right former President Mbeki and thank you for your openness and honesty, together with the best in the world we too are prone to pettiness, petulance, selfishness and short-sightedness. I sit and wonder how embarrassing it must be for our elders who have since passed on to see their legacy turned upside down by the ones they entrusted and had hoped they would take this glorious nation to greater heights. I am referring to the class of OR Tambo, a class of true leadership, which boasted Mbeki's own father. I urge you not to open the Pandora box, it scares me like Dracula does, or perhaps the Pandora box your own skeletons are in is made of a different piece of steel, one that cannot be opened or broken. I am sure you do have your own skeletons, no doubt about it, as you threaten a Pandora box I am sure there's more of your own skeletons in that box than any other's.

I sit and wonder about the Pandora's box that you were referring to; Just wondering of the connection between Jackie Selebi's (may his soul rest in perfect peace) corruption story and the rape and corruption case against Zuma which is startling. I keep asking myself why Lucky Dube would sing about these things, and as if the sequence was directed by Anant Singh in a movie titled South Africa after the leadership of Nelson Mandela. In his song, Crime and Corruption, who are the real perpetrators of crime and corruption? Is it not the leaders themselves, I wonder? I get chills on my spine having to think of what my glorious nation's surprise would be, the next scandal, the next embarrassment. From where I'm sitting I wonder if this is what the black struggle is about? We understand there are always differences in leadership – it doesn't matter if it is between once very close friends or comrades – but I

128

know leaders are also very smart and wise enough. But what should make the South African leadership very special is that they have to continue the legacy of a great leadership and not make a mockery of it. Whatever it is, can it be sorted out as decently as possible? To leaders of a party who have seen our emancipation from white dominance, can I just be blunt and ask, if Steve Biko and Chris Hani were still alive, what would they say? They held different ideologies and weren't from the same party but they fought against the same cause. And you carry on and fight within yourselves. What about the many people who died for this cause, not forgetting our brothers and sisters who endured hardships in exile for the same? Like, if this is happening today, what does the future hold for us? What would any future South African leader say to us as a nation that will help rebuild this nation after this drama? Is this it? Do you realise that we are slowly losing confidence in our own people? Are you small boys that you could be conducting yourselves like this? After overcoming obstacles to achieve the majority vote, is this it? Who can we trust to lead our country to the next level? Will you blame our children if they refer to you inappropriately because they won't understand today's politics tomorrow? Because I don't understand either. What about your legacies, the both of you, I wonder? The ANC house doesn't seem to be in order; there are just too many decisions made and changed. I wonder what it's like going into those Executive meetings where serious issues are debated and decisions taken. For the sake of the many South Africans who perished before this day, please forever keep your peace. This is not about you; it's about a nation that is still licking its wounds from the oppression, from the brutality, from the humiliation of a system called Apartheid.

I come from a humble family background and had to work as soon as I finished my matric (today's Grade 12) with no experience or exposure whatsoever. My mother was a domestic worker and couldn't afford college fees; my father worked as a packer for one of South Africa's supermarkets. In 1987, as a young girl who was naïve and ignorant of the state of our country then, I was blessed and got employed by the South African Council of Churches. I never enjoyed my job as we were constantly harassed by the security forces. I had no choice and had to stay on, despite the fact that my peers were either enjoying college, or their work, and I wasn't when I should have been. I know the price others had to pay for believing that what they were fighting for was a worthy cause. I know that; I have seen it with my own eyes. I didn't expect this mediocre power struggle in this day and time. It's almost unbelievable that this is happening in South Africa. I didn't know that power does this to those that are in it, and overtaken by it, and I have always believed that leaders surround themselves with people who are able to guide them. Where are these people? My experience is that they are in it for themselves, that's it. They get paid by the state, enjoy their benefits, and don't give a flying monkey about what is right for our country.

It is for that reason that most of our leaders have their own people – they go with those leaders wherever they are deployed– it doesn't matter if they are experts in these new areas, or not. It's not about what people know, but about the person they are with. People are made to serve personalities and not the cause. Where are we going as a nation? I have known the ruling party to be a noble organisation; or is there something we are missing? In Guns and Roses Lucky mentions why, after just five years of being in power, we have now become a nation that looks at the colour of our flags. Formerly, it was the colour of our skins. Our nation will be destroyed by ourselves, and he is very explicit about this truth. He said this when our democracy was just five years old; sixteen years later, when we should have been growing stronger together, we are weak and divided.

Fighting the apartheid regime wasn't an easy thing. We stood together as one; side by side, we were brothers yesterday when our mouths were shut by the system, but today when the world cares to listen to us, all they can hear is our loud fighting, crime and corruption. If the world were to start singing with us, would the song be in Xhosa or Zulu … I'm just wondering? Sometimes my little grey matter and imagination run away with me. If the person succeeding Mbeki had been Xhosa, would we have this drama? Or would the succession have been smooth and timeously as planned? With no power struggle? I surprise myself with my thoughts at times. My point is this: as a South African, I should be able to support a leader appointed for the reasons that they are appointed, which should, by the way, be shared with the nation. To the many South Africans –including those that have been destroyed by their own – please stop separating us; we love our country. The Bible says 'He made man in His image' but it didn't say black or white, Zulu or Xhosa – Different Colours One People. Can we embrace our beautiful South Africa and fight together towards a common cause? Let's rather fight climate change and come up with solutions that will save our planet for the generations after us. Or how about we fight Mr HIV/AIDS together – we have enough common enemies to fight – or don't we?

Whoever thought this succession plan would work out, and recommended it, must be eating humble pie and digesting it very slowly. How can you forget that when you were underground working day and night, you had a common enemy to fight? Today we destroy even the smartest people who've been to the highest learning institutions because someone appoints them and makes them their pet, and then when that leader goes, the skilled person goes with them, just like that! Skills and expertise clearly don't seem to matter - it's more about whose side you're on rather than whether your skills can make a positive difference where you are or not. We are all South African – this country belongs to all of us. Don't be blinded by the fact that there might be others who don't agree with you, who might also want to go underground for the same reasons. We don't need that in South Africa today. In fact, if it was possible to rewind until the period when Nelson Mandela was the leader, compress and burn the years thereafter, and then elect new leaders who were willing to lead with integrity, wouldn't it be wonderful? You have made a mockery of our democracy – period, full stop. You need to stop. This is our government, you are leaders in it and you are not indispensable. Let us create and support true African leaders, who will lead with integrity, we follow and give them our support because this is our government. Being a true African is an honourable thing, Lucky was a true African hero, proudly so. In the words of Mama Miriam Makeba, my leaders "with your wisdom gather all the young for me, black cloud hanging over nest your bosom strong and free, guard each gallant warriors' claim, cause I'm the soil from which they came, spread your glory, sunshine and unify my promised land".

6. HIS CAREER

Apart from his music and the issues expressed in his music, Lucky never complained of government support or lack of work in South Africa. When the international markets opened, he took his career to the next level and emulated successful musicians of our time. He treated his career with respect and honoured every opportunity he was given. In my early days of working with him, I remember discussing the year planner with him and must have said something like, "Then after the US tour we will be playing at such and such a place on such a date...?" He paused and asked me if I was in it to play? That was a funny question; I mean the music industry term for performing is playing. That's what I've always known and others never had a problem with the terminology. He brought me to order right there and told me to say that we will be working at such and such on this date. The man took his career that seriously; he knew he wasn't playing but working.

When he travelled to Africa, there would be no fewer than sixteen of us travelling with him. Ten musicians on stage, a monitor engineer, a front of house engineer, a tour manager, two roadies and myself. He wouldn't take a chance on his live performance being engineered by someone who wasn't familiar with his songs. He had seen too many good career musicians go down because their recorded songs were different from their live performance. To this day people wonder how his band managed to keep the same quality and standard. With the rest of the world, he managed with only eleven on the road, because his road manager for the other territories was also an engineer and played both roles. The roadie was also American and it was easier to do their paperwork (work permits) for the other territories..

It was a rule that if someone couldn't afford performance fees, then we didn't take the show. This was so that the person wouldn't be burdened, and also so that those dicey promoters wouldn't be tempted to take chances, which often led them to disappearing after the shows! When things don't go right, the artist also doesn't feel right. When you know what the other person lost in terms of flights, fees and other logistics, you can't feel right about it. Live shows require a lot of marketing and publicity all the time. I don't care if you're a Michael Jackson (may his soul rest in peace) brand or anything better than that. For some odd reason the promoters would think that the name Lucky Dube was such a strong brand that all they would need to do was put up a few posters and people would be convinced the show would happen. Often, a day before the show, we would be expected to parade him in a motorcade trying to cover as much ground as possible, and this would go on the whole day! This irritated him a lot. We were in a Jeep once in Freetown, Sierra Leone, doing this parade when we were almost carried away by the masses who decided they would carry the Jeep up high. I was terrified, and the look in Lucky's eyes was saying we've got to get out of this. The fans themselves caused huge problems, following us through to the hotel where they would camp just to catch a glimpse of him. Professional promoters would do everything in their power to promote the shows aggressively and spent money on marketing. This is what people forget in the entertainment industry; you'll know by the level of promotion if a show will be a success or not. People aren't ignorant; they know that sometimes even credible promoters fail at the last minute because of this or that technicality. It's showbiz, after all! Lucky understood the importance of commitment from the promoter's side. His terms of engagement seemed impossible to meet, but once a promoter could meet them he knew it was going to be worth it for both parties. He was strict about the contract – not a penny more not a penny less, and this is what sustained his business.

We faced many challenges; it wasn't all that easy. He lost a lot of money along the way but the show went on. He let me make mistakes so I could learn. One such mistake happened when the promoter told me that he only had a certain amount of money for the second show. Instead of consulting with Lucky, I agreed to the amount that the promoter claimed he had. Lucky told me later, "You see, you've just been stitched up, this happens all the time. They do that knowing that you can't cancel the second show when you're already there!" I was a miserable person that weekend and I mean it. I locked myself in my room and cried and kicked myself for being that stupid! Why hadn't I consulted Lucky first? I wondered if he believed me or if he thought I'd made the story up? I received counselling from him later on, red eyes, puffy face and all. He didn't stop there; he told me many stories of previous scams and he showed me the blind spots of the game. I got it. But still I felt bad. I vowed never to repeat that mistake in my life. He told me promoters are like taxi drivers – they behave the same all over the world. It seems there's one big Training School for Baddies out there.

One of the amazing things about him was that he managed to keep a consistent band, which is a very rare thing. Bands are difficult to keep together; people are on and off all the time. Lucky's band was always tight and this wasn't because he was an angel to work for. His rules of engagement were clear from day one: no stories after the shows – they all shared stories of how difficult it was after spending more than a month on the road – he would rather deal with issues that didn't affect his band. It was okay for the first two weeks but thereafter you were easily irritated by the person next to you. Lucky had to keep it together under those difficult circumstances. I personally was never on the road with him and the band for more than two weeks, and I know I was already agitated by the first week!

7. THE LEGACY

Having survived his childhood which was probably as tough as the bullets that destroyed him, when he departed from this world he didn't leave it the same way he found it. He left something valuable behind through his music; he made a mark no one will ever be able to erase. He was born poor but at the time of his death he had it all, and even more than he'd ever imagined. He affected situations and people, both positively and negatively. He irritated those who hated the truth, so I guess he affected them negatively with a positive message! Those who loved peace he affected positively with the truth. He never claimed to be this or that, but he was many things and all of them good. He passed wisdom, experience and knowledge on to the many people who crossed his path.

He had a mysteriously good effect on some people, in quite bizarre situations. For instance, once when he was performing in Fiji, the local prisoners were allowed to go and watch his concert. Afterwards, instead of attempting to escape, they all took themselves back to the prison! On another occasion, someone started shooting randomly because he was emotional about Lucky's music. Luckily, nothing bad happened. Some cried when they saw Lucky perform, some shouted, some thought of him as some power they couldn't explain. The many thousands of fans were amazing and scary at the same time; we couldn't deal with the fan club requests that we received on a daily basis. His admirers were extremely loyal even though he didn't know them personally. But they all felt that they knew him somehow, sharing his messages of peace, love and unity which of course is what the whole world needs. Some of them told Lucky how, after listening to his music, they were delivered from their troubles. Some testified that their marriages were restored after seeing him in concert; some indicated that they approached life differently after listening to this or that track. They basically gave praise to Lucky for their successes in all areas of their lives, and I'm talking about thousands of testimonies.

These gestures disturbed Lucky very much. I got to understand the testimonies after he involved me in his fan club quarterly newsletters which we produced together for the fans. I had to read all the letters and respond to some of them. The letters were very personal but there was one thing in common – most people experienced an inner peace throughout his performances. And it lasted way beyond the performance; his fans would express their gratitude for the effect he had on them long after. In fact, it's an understatement to say people's lives were changed by his music; he influenced positive change in people's lives without even realising it.

He would worry about the future messages that he had to send out. You see, Lucky understood that he was already living his purpose in life, he didn't have to still figure it out.

The effect he had on me personally when he went on stage was riveting. He would become someone I didn't know. I got chills up and down my spine each time people treated him like royalty. This proved to me that God knows the plans he has for us; we don't have to be born to a certain family to receive the attention and respect of the world. The attention Lucky Dube got around the world was very special; he said it was unnecessary and undeserved but I know differently. If God gives one man the talent to write and sing to His people and his music has the effect it had on those people, then I know that it was all the hand of Jah Almighty.

Today we live in a world where we worry about how much money we can make each year, how many times we are able to change our cars, what sort of areas we live in, but we forget the small things – like the effect we have on others. What sort of effect do you have on your colleagues, relatives, neighbours and society at large? How many of our departed friends and relatives still have an effect on us; how do we remember them? I ask myself how I would like to be remembered when I'm gone. It is a heavy, serious question …

Lucky needed no reasons to have a positive effect on others; he just needed to be himself.

Those who killed Lucky Dube are wrong if they think they killed his message; his legacy lives on. In his lifetime he created jobs, he contributed directly and indirectly to the livelihood of many families, he remains an icon in the creative industry of Southern Africa. He has been an ambassador for South Africa for many years; his legacy is bigger than anyone can comprehend.

Although Lucky was influenced by the late Peter Tosh, he made sure that his Reggae was unique to South African sounds; he created a legacy for himself. Reggae was born in Jamaica but Lucky revolutionized it and took it to another level. His was to become one of the very appealing styles of Reggae that set him apart from the rest. He didn't want to be another Peter Tosh, although he liked his style. Lucky sang for the world but he didn't lose his African identity. He came with a strong, spellbinding style and his audiences ate out of the palm of his hand all the time.

Considering how hard it is to write a groundbreaking song, let alone a reggae song, I ask myself this simple albeit difficult question: what made it so simple and easy for him to write such sensible and moving songs? He left behind some wonderful stories for us to remember him by. Is this the guy who said, "people have had troubles from since the Dead Sea was only critical"? Is he the same guy who said, "we've all had problems since the time the pope was an altar boy?" Only Lucky would have thought of the pope being an altar boy at some point in his life, or to think of our problems being as ancient as the critical sea to the point of it dying? I consider myself to have been blessed to have met and been a part of this super human being. His is a story that is worth my breath and, believe you me, I understand how important my breath is!

The most amazing things have happened during my journey with this great man. He once showed me a passport picture of myself, which he'd apparently picked up from my office during one of his visits. This picture was kept in his wallet with that of his "mother," Freda Lowe, and his daughter Laura. I had no idea he had my picture nor how long he'd kept it. In his office he had another picture of me on the wall, together with one of Laura. Was this gesture just one of those things that happen in life or should I try and find a spiritual meaning? As I write this book I pray for spiritual guidance; I believe there has to be a reason.

One of my most significant memories that I will forever cherish, was when he told me I was a special person. Not special to him personally but that there was something about me that others didn't have, and he asked if I was aware of it. I was genuinely surprised because I truly wasn't aware of any such thing! I thought to myself at the time that he was trying to charm me, but then he went on and said, "just be consistent with your values and faith in what you say for the world to hear, but most importantly what you say that only you and God know."

I thought he was just being a brother who didn't want to see my character destroyed by the things we go through in life. There were two of us that he felt this way about. Lucky had this thing about the late Bhekumuzi Luthuli, a Maskandi musician who has since passed on. May his soul rest in peace. Lucky loved Bhekumuzi in a very amazing way. The connection between us as humans is amazing; we realise later on in life that the people we have strong feelings for have a natural connection to us and therefore a divine meaning. I know why I had this connection with Lucky – I had to learn.

I was deeply touched by a newspaper write-up after the One People band's performance at Moretele Park 2011 Tribute to the Legends concert. It felt as if the journalist was reading the minds of so many people all over the world when he summed up Lucky's legacy in a very moving article:

"My therapeutic moment came when the Lucky Dube Band took the stage at Moretele Park in Mamelodi on Saturday night. Earlier in the day, I had listened to Mogoeng trying to convince himself and

fellow South Africans that he was the best judicial mind that this country had ever produced.

"He consistently sought to convince himself and all of us that he is capable of being a leader among leading judges who, through their

judgments, will be able to make the law that should be followed by the rest of the judiciary.

"I had begun to review the bar that distinguishes excellence from mediocrity in this country. It needed some adjustments to remove the shock in me so that when Mogoeng is finally appointed, as he probably will be, I will be ready to join in celebrating a truly South African achievement.

"You just have to love our country's ability to spot talented leaders! As Archbishop Desmond Tutu would say in a different context, we are an amazing people. Really amazing.

"So, when the Lucky Dube Band took to the stage, I witnessed a genuine legacy in action, a legacy to be proud of.

"The enthusiasm with which people danced to Lucky Dube's classic tunes – Feel Irie, Racial Discrimination, Prisoner, among others – testified to a positive legacy Dube bequeathed. Here was a band replaying with precision – minus the original lead vocalist – Dube's uniquely South African reggae.

"Revellers, including myself, could only reciprocate. The band got a resounding reception similar to, if not a little more than, that accorded to the legendary and forever youthful 70-something-year-old Hugh Masekela.

"The fact that the band has stayed united after merciless thugs robbed us of Dube's life is an indication of the bonds he created among its members.

"It's a legacy of real leadership. The consistent theme of unity in

diversity contained in his songs continues to resonate not only amongb his millions of fans, but also within his own band.

"His political tunes aimed at the brutal apartheid regime are still sung with the same zeal as they were back in the days when they were produced and topped the music charts. More significantly, unlike many Struggle songs which have since been vulgarised, with lyrics changed to insult present leaders, Dube's songs don't seem to lend themselves to such.

"The background vocalists still do their thing – that which I remember seeing them do in Dube's DVD, recorded live in Uganda. The Moretele crowd responded the same way as the Ugandan crowd.

"Dube was a truly international artist. In many music shops his albums are found in different categories – 'reggae' and 'world music'. After he was killed, his obituary appeared in newspapers of international repute, including The Economist.

"Well, some might correctly pozint out that many obituaries, including PW Botha's and Adolf Hitler's, had been published in international newspapers. So in itself it is not a credit. True. What matters is what is said in those obituaries.

"Dube was always and correctly portrayed as a voice of reason pre- and post-apartheid. Moretele bore testimony to his enduring legacy.

"Beyond the indelible mark he left behind through his music, spiced with skanking guitars and drums, Dube left behind (I hope I don't get into trouble for saying this), an extraordinarily beautiful daughter.

"Bongi Dube briefly took part in the performance, unleashing a powerful rendition of a tribute to her father. He could have been a king born in a palace; to her, he was 'my daddy'. He could have been many things to many people; to her he was 'my daddy'.
142

"Bongi's beauty, I concluded, must have radiated from her inside. And she was right, Dube meant many things to many people, but they all were united by his messages of unity".

When I read this article I thought: well, I'm not the only person who understands the legacy of this great man. I'm honoured and deeply touched that South Africans truly know what they had and are not afraid to appreciate at this level.

8. LIFE TOO SHORT?

Is life too short? as the saying goes. I sometimes think that if I had spent one more day with Lucky maybe he would have told me this or that. If I hadn't been dodging whenever he needed someone to chat to, maybe I could have learnt a little more than I have.

But in reality I think life is too short for those of us whose contribution towards humankind is of a selfish nature. Life wasn't too short for Lucky Dube. He lived to the age of 43 but his contributions far exceeded many others who live to be 100. Contribution towards humankind is not only financial; teachers might be the highest contributors in any society but we forget about them once we are in good positions or become wealthy.

Their responsibility is to teach the nation but you find them amongst the poor, depending on their pensions when they can no longer teach. Only a few will retire comfortably because they did this or that to augment their income. I have chosen teachers as a subject because I'm touched by how most of them end up in life, and yet their contribution towards humankind is immeasurable. Their wisdom and teachings eventually produce the scientists, lawyers, doctors, and so on who are the foundation of our nation. Life is too short when the life lived was wasted on unimportant things. Lucky Dube's life was not too short; we continue to think that he could have contributed more if he had lived just another day. That is an emotional statement, but looking at what he has left in the archives of the music industry, his was a full life. Looking at the footsteps he has left in the whole African continent, his was a life lived to the fullest. I have often wondered what is going to happen to all the published material he left behind. He took time to observe, to think, to apply his opinion without fear and I speculate: did he stand in front of his mirror and practise his steps or pace around his house humming the tunes, taking his cows to graze but also talking to them? What was this man made of that I am still not getting since he has gone?

Once when I was talking to him he was out whistling to his cows at the same time as he answered the phone, and I had to tell him that stage dancing and sweating, and whistling at cows, are worlds apart! He laughed at me. Who would have imagined Lucky taking an interest in anything except his music? But his life was balanced. I want to talk about plans for the year and he is talking to his cows. He spoke about his cows as if he were referring to humans; he had respect for them, he was connected to them and they were important to him. He employed three people on his farm to take care of the 'cow business' but he still made time to attend to them and give them his attention.

I can hear Lucky say, "tell them Rasta, my life was not too short, there was nothing else I had to offer on earth. I played my part and I have to move to greater things. I have just moved to another level. I am now in the spirit world. I consider life to be too short only if wasted on useless things." When I hear the things that people all over the world have to say about Lucky, I am comforted to know that his messages will be relevant for many years to come. The reminder is always there. I stumbled on an article written by Abel Dzobo, a journalist and filmmaker born from Zimbabwe who is currently a Senior Sub-Editor with The Herald, the Zimpapers (1980) Ltd flagship daily newspaper in Zimbabwe. A fan of music, he is greatly inspired by Lucky Dube, and he has written many articles about him. This is what he wrote about Lucky in October 2012:

"LAST Thursday was the fifth anniversary of iconic South African reggae musician, Lucky Dube's death. Dube was gunned down in a carjack attempt at the age of 43.

Born on August 3 1964 and with 22 albums under his belt, Dube won a plethora of regional and international awards. A great fighter against apartheid and racism, and after independence, crime and corruption in South Africa, crime ironically claimed his life.

146

But many things have happened ever since, the most recent being the Marikana massacre.

This saw 34 strikers gunned down by South African police in Marikana as they demanded a pay rise.

But what would Lucky Dube say about such a massacre?

Lucky Dube believed in peace and harmony, and the sacredness of human life.

And be it the police or miners, all are victims as depicted in Dube's song "Victims".

But little did he know that, Eventually the enemy, Will stand aside and look, While we slash and kill, Our own brothers, Knowing that already,

They are the victims of the situation.

Was the strike justified? The issue of empowerment of the indigenous people is getting topical by the day on the African and Latin American continents. The South African miners wanted an increase in their salaries, which were way below the Poverty Datum Line.

Also, instead of handouts, they wanted to become masters of their own destinies, that is, through running the economy itself. Lucky Dube

captures this in the song "Hungry Free Man" off the album "Taxman" (1997).

What is the point in being free, When you can't get no job, What is the point in being free, When you can't get food, What is the point in going out to work, When others can get for free, What

is the point in being free, When you don't have no home, Do you

147

wanna be, A well fed slave or a hungry free man?

Black South Africans were discriminated against during apartheid. They could not go to school, as Dube sings in "Slave, 1989", which is also the title of the album.

They won't build no schools anymore, All they'll build will be prisons, prison.

But since a majority government in 1994, government has invested much into education, building schools and according to the School Realities Report (2011) South Africa has 25 851 schools. However, the majority of South Africans are not learned, with a meagre 88 percent literacy rate and sitting at number 144 in the world, according to the United Nations Development

Programme (2011) report. Though Black Economic Empowerment (BEE) was launched by the government to redress the inequalities of apartheid, giving previously disadvantaged groups (black Africans, Coloureds, Indians and some Chinese) employment preference,

skills development, ownership, management, socio-economic development, and preferential procurement, few blacks can utilise it.

Lucky Dube pulls no punches, South Africans just have to go to school, as in the song "Affirmative Action" off the album "Trinity" (1995).

You blamed it on apartheid, You blamed it on the government and everybody, Now is the time to prove yourself, Constitution can be changed, But that does not mean that, You don't need no education, We are tired of people who, Think that affirmative action is the way out, And, is another way of putting puppets, Where they don't belong.

148

So the strike was justified, but not attacking policemen. Just by staying at home, the miners would have ensured zero productivity, and the Lonmin management would have been forced onto the negotiating table.

But the miners armed themselves with guns, spears, knives and knobkerries and advanced on the police details. They had even killed two policemen days before. In the song "Crime and Corruption", off the album "The Way It Is" (1999), Dube blasts government for doing nothing when police officers are gunned down in broad daylight.

Policemen get killed everyday, And you say it is not that bad, Maybe if you see it through the eyes, Of the victims, You will join us and fight this, Crime and corruption.

Then comes the issue of consulting a traditional healer, a sangoma. Is it part of South African culture? Dube says its normal for South Africans to consult a sangoma in the song "Julie Julie" off the album "The Other Side" (2003).

He lives up on the mountain, They say he mixes herbs, Throws the bones, tells the future, I'm on my way right now, I wanna know about my future, With a girl named Julie.

Unlike Nigerian movies that vilify traditional healers, Dube defends them in the song "Julie, Julie."

Some people call him a witchdoctor, But how can he be a witch and a doctor at the same time?

Nonetheless, the belief that the sangoma's medicine could turn bullets into water is something

Dube would have scoffed at. It last happened in 1905, the Maji Maji Rebellion of Tanzania as they fought German colonialists.

149

A spirit medium named Kinjikitile Ngwale claimed to be possessed by a snake spirit called Hongo and began calling himself "Bokero."

The bullets never turned into water, so the Tanzanians were defeated. So for the South African miners to repeat the mistake of 1905 is mind-

boggling. Maybe as they say, "history repeats itself." Dube sings in the song "Crazy World" off the album "House of Exile" (1991).

But we don't know what tomorrow brings, In this crazy world, People dying like flies every day, You read about it in the news, But you don't believe it.

Despite South Africa having a black government, still the policemen and miners were gunned down.

This ties in with Dube's song, "My Brother My Enemy" off the album "Trinity" (1995).

I'm a living witness, now I know that . . .Not every black man is my brother, Not every white man is my enemy.

Forty men died during the Marikana massacre, leaving behind women to take care of the children.

Dube captures in the song "God Bless the Women" on the album "Trinity" (1995).

She prayed for her children, She prayed for their education, Then she prayed for the man, That left her with her children.We, praise heroes everyday, But there are those that we forget To praise, The women of this world.

So Lucky Dube had the last words, Respect is the golden virtue. If the Lonmin Mine management respected the miners, then there would never have been a strike. If the striking miners respected the police, they would not have attacked them.

They would not have looked for a sangoma to turn bullets into water.

The miners would not have been shot.

Respect is Lucky Dube's last album (2006).

9. LUCKY DIES

I had just woken up in a hotel room in Botswana where I'd been attending an exhibition. I'm not a morning person but that morning was particularly slow as we'd hosted a dinner the previous night. We had already started marketing the much-awaited South African Soccer World Cup 2010. One of our objectives was to sell the opportunities available in South Africa to the SADC region and we'd invited the Sports fraternity of the Botswana Government to a dinner we would host on 18 October 2007. Dinner went very well; we achieved what we had set out to achieve in Botswana and the next few days we continued at the exhibition site.

I stumbled around that morning, trying to recover from the previous night. I switched on my mobile phone which had been off since dinner the previous night, and listened to the voice messages. But the strange thing was that there were just irritated sounds of people who obviously didn't want to leave me a message, but needed to tell me something. As I tried to listen to the background of the dropped messages I heard chaos, as if the people who were calling were in a crowd or driving in a very noisy place. The last message was from my partner asking that I call him urgently. I could sense something was very wrong and as I tried to dial his number I felt very uneasy, almost shaky. He answered his phone and asked if I was okay. Haltingly, I told him I was okay, but with a query in my voice. And then he baldly told me he had bad news for me. Feeling queasy, I asked what it was. He paused and then said quietly, "Lucky has been shot." My heart racing, I said, "is he okay?" And then came the impossible, unendurable words, "No, he didn't make it…." My head felt full of cotton wool. I repeated, "You said Lucky was shot, Lucky who?" And he answered, "Lucky Dube."

I've heard bad news before, but nothing prepared me for this one. I felt as if I'd been kicked in my solar plexus – all the breath knocked out of me. I didn't ask him what had happened or anything after

153

that; my mind said he was talking nonsense. I dropped the phone to call Mandla Nene, Lucky's assistant. We both worked with Lucky at the time. Mandla manned the office and was Lucky's confidante on all levels. He picked up the phone and, hearing my voice, started crying, "Lenah mfowethu" (Lenah my sister), that's all Mandla could say to me.

Lucky, you were dead wrong to say "Big Boys Don't Cry." Mandla couldn't handle seeing the lifeless body of the man he'd seen a few hours earlier having been wasted like that; he was destroyed inside. Pain and hurt cannot describe how Mandla felt. I hadn't heard the details of the story at this point, just the unreal reality that Lucky was gone. Mandla couldn't tell me what had happened, he was overcome by emotion. I felt as if I was walking upstream against a strong current, getting nowhere. I would be lying if I said I felt pain or hurt myself; something just overtook me – probably shock. I thought I was going crazy; I thought I was dreaming. There was no one to confirm what I'd been told; I was in a hotel room all by myself. It's been said that nothing tests us like death; I have seen and experienced it. I am not the fainting type but at that moment I wished I could have fainted just to take a break from the awful gaping hole of confusion, and then wake up to a different reality. I looked at myself in the mirror and confirmed this was me. I don't know what there is about mirrors but it helped trigger a scream. I screamed and then I started crying, and then my mind started functioning.

I had travelled to Botswana with two colleagues, Barba Gaoganediwe whom I reported to and Sipho Shoyisa a colleague from another department . I called them screaming. It was Barba who thought I was suffering a panic attack of some sort, in that early the morning! He called the hotel personnel for assistance before he could come to my room. The hotel personnel and my colleagues arrived in my room to find me in a terrible state. I was shaking. I felt dizzy and confused. I wanted to run and at the same time felt very weak. None of them had heard the news. I broke the news to them, and Barba then reached for me, and held me tight. I held on to this man so tight I wouldn't let go; I was trembling. I thought I was going to die but I was wrong – a death doesn't kill you, it makes you strong. I'd only been working with Barba for a little over a year and we had a strange working relationship. It wasn't the kind that shared hugs, but that day I held on to him like a leech. He asked someone to bring sugared water for me; I think that's when I was able to sit down and open my eyes to this terrible reality.

It was inevitable that I would be taken back to the same pain of two years before when my mother was murdered in the comfort of her own home. When my mother died I felt I died with her; now I died with Lucky all over again. I thought: the world is only pain to me, my faith is gone, I hate life.

My two colleagues were both aware of my involvement in the life of Lucky Dube. In fact, on our way to Botswana, Sipho and I sattogether in the flight and had a chat and he related how he'd almost worked with Lucky at some point in his life. He had been on a mentoring program for young trainees in the technical side of the music industry. I'd then shared the moving details of my journey with Lucky, little knowing that in two days I would be referring to him as the late Lucky Dube.

My boss then arranged that I travel back to South Africa on the next available flight.. Everything appeared as irrational and unreal as a dream; everything was happening so fast and yet so slowly. I felt as if I was in a nightmare and desperately wanted someone to wake me up before the dream became reality. This was to become a permanent wish. I had just lost a friend, a brother, a shining star, a jewel, my spiritual mentor, my inspiration. Did my colleagues even understand what I was going through, as they found themselves in this unreal reality of my situation?

I met Lucky Dube in 1995 when I joined Gallo Record Company as a secretary in the legal department. He was signed to Gallo as a recording artist and recorded many albums with them. I would see him walk through the passages and all would gather around him and give him this unnecessary attention. It seemed very strange to me; I didn't really like his music and this attention didn't make sense to me.

I moved positions in 1996 from the legal department to the unit that promoted and marketed South African music outside of South Africa, and that was when I got to interact with the man himself. I started as a Personal Assistant to the head of that unit, Antos Stella, a position I held for less than six months. She promoted me to Marketing Assistant where I was able to have direct interaction with the artists. It was not until he brought his daughter to the office that Lucky and I made a connection. I love children very much and was pregnant with my third daughter. He would come to the office and spend time in my office and tease me about my pregnancy which at first he thought was my first. I liked the way he behaved, always sharing his stories with me, but what moved me the most was his dedication to his children. I wonder what the world would be like if some fathers were like him. I was later on given a position as an Artist Development and Liaison Manager in the same unit, a position that afforded me the opportunity to travel with the artists and go to International exhibitions to market and promote them. I was then given the responsibility of securing shows outside of South Africa; Lucky was one of the artists.

At first the shows would be secured by the unit head and then I would deal with the travel logistics, visas, etc. and, at a later stage, when her responsibilities were increasing, I had to take over and do the business. My career was at its peak; I travelled the world and the more I travelled, the harder I worked. I got on very well with my boss, who mentored me through my journey in the music industry. I shared her friends too. She rewarded hard work when it was due and she and I worked like partners, developing one of the strongest bonds you can ever find. She'd seen me through a lot in my life; I've also been there as a sister when things were rough in hers.

When she entrusted me with the careers of these artists she knew

156

they were in good hands, and she would still oversee the smooth running of things in the department.

Life is really strange; when you grow career-wise there are those who are negatively affected. I found myself having to step into her shoes just like that and some of the artists weren't happy about it. But this was a reality no one could change. It was hard at first for them to trust that I would service them the way she'd been servicing them. She was very good at customer relations, and wouldn't mix business with pleasure. I am good with interpersonal relations, but still had to learn to draw the line. I was new in the business, I had to learn fast. Lucky, like many other artists, felt neglected; at the same time there was this new kid on the block trying to impress and my new energy seemed to work for me. They soon had to learn to work and trust this new kid on the block.

I travelled the continent with Lucky. Apart from the amazing crowds that he would move, his music would make you want to search your soul and correct any issues you might find hidden there. I cried a lot when he got on stage; I looked at his audience, made up mostly of the poorest of the poor. Lucky represented the masses. He had told me his story as a youth growing up in poverty, but nothing prepared me for his impact. Having known his struggles I failed to understand how his music could have such ramifications on so many souls. I sometimes wished those very masses could know his own struggles. I knew his story, I watched his moving performances, I saw the poverty around us, and I cried and cried. So as my colleagues drove me to the airport on that terrible day, I wondered if they had the slightest idea of what I was going through – I had just lost Lucky.

Flights on that Friday were so full, I was the 13th person on the waiting list. But as soon as the staff at the airport heard the reason why I had to get home, my status on that waiting list was immediate priority. I became priority. Me. You see, Lucky Dube was the son of the soil. I have been treated like royalty before, so this didn't come as a surprise but was somewhat expected because I was an associate of Lucky Dube. I was handled with care – like I was delicate – and seriously this was the only time I enjoyed my 'important' status. I was going through this unreal reality that Lucky was gone and I still didn't have the details, except that he was killed in a botched hijacking.

My flight from Botswana was the longest I'd ever taken in my life. We finally landed in South Africa and I stumbled through the airport to find my partner waiting for me. He said nothing to me, and I said nothing to him. We just drove to the office, where I found people waiting. The office was full of friends and associates who had been gathering to hear what had happened. I felt weak at my knees. I was trembling but I gathered the strength to go inside. I fell to the ground as I saw the devastation in the familiar faces looking at me.

At the time when I should be having hotel breakfast in Botswana I had one special breakfast that morning. One I will remember for the rest of my life, my moment of being served

BULLETS FOR BREAKFAST (poem)

I had breakfast one unforgettable morning

Served to me forcefully

A breakfast I had to have no matter what

A breakfast different from any other

Special in its nature I had to eat it,

Forcefully as my throat suffered greatly to swallow

This breakfast so special and yet so difficult

Different presentation , but not new to me

I had had different breakfasts before

Served to me in the morning and I got acquainted

To the different breakfasts life serves me

When the room service knock came

I tried to brush my teeth before the breakfast

But then again I decided there was no need

No need at all to brush your teeth

For this special breakfast I only am acquainted

All I needed was to put my brace napkin

To make sure my breast and all that is in it

Is protected, covered in a napkin

Like the soldiers cover themselves in

breast plate in a war

So do I cover my breast in a special napkin

A napkin trusted enough to protect the

Steel turned heart of this strong black woman

For I only am acquainted to the special

Breakfast, not so many people are invited to

This napkin stays on my breast

Now that the girls have sucked

Each one of them, their last drop

Of the natural juices mother earth offered

Pure in its form, it's always been

Its reliability is unbelievable as

It always assures me, of how strong I am

That no matter how strong the stain

From the breakfast, the beat goes on

As I approached my serving that morning

I wasn't sure what to expect

My last special breakfast

Looked cold, and unappetizing

Complicated in its presentation

To this day I am still baffled

I had to approach the special serving anyway

Accepting an offering life served me, I could not refuse

Accepting that life always serves me what I do not order

I approached the breakfast anyway

When my special breakfast was served,

There was no one to whisper to, no one to scream to

To ask if indeed this was my breakfast

Landing straight, into my heart

Forgetting I had a stomach

No tea cold or warm

No dashing of a drink of sorts or straight, or on the rocks

No buttered bread

No fried nor scrambled eggs

Straight from my sleep

I had to eat my breakfast

Three bullets

Served on a platter, hard and cold, in a hotel room

Room service it had to be, no starter no desert

Special I've always known that I was

The breakfast was over special

For I could not handle the honor

Of this particular special breakfast

Three bullets

On who

Lucky what

What did you say again

Which Lucky are you talking about

As my special breakfast was getting into my system

I got drunk from just the three bullets

So drunk my world was spinning

Spinning with confusion

Spinning with hate

Spinning with fear

Spinning with hurt

Spinning with grief

Spinning with pain

Spinning with resentment

Bullets for breakfast

The bullets that still make my world spin

Bullets that kept me drunk for many years

Bullets that kept me addicted for many years

Bullets that kept me obsessed for many years

Bullets that kept me cold for many years

Bullets for breakfast

I hate you with a hate

I hate you with a hate from my heart,

liver, lungs, oesophagus, large intestines,

small intestines, my blood,brain, hair, eyes, nose,

mouth, cheeks , ears, neck, my feet, legs, my toes,

nails and everything I am made of.

Bullets for breakfast I wish I could pee on you.

Bullets for breakfast I wish I could fart on you,

Bullets for breakfast I wish I could send you

To where you came from in the first place

For we don't need you in Africa

As I swallowed my breakfast made of bullets in a familiar environment, Lucky's office, another round of sugared water to wash down the pain. I took a breath and looked at Mandla in disbelief. It was at this point that I realized that my earlier wish was just that, a wish; it was then confirmed Lucky was no more. In one of his songs Lucky wrote: "If I am dreaming, don't wake me up, if it is a lie, don't tell me the truth, cause what the truth will do, it's gonna hurt my heart." I wished I had been in a dream, but I was there in his office, the very office where we held meetings, did so many newsletters; the owner was no more. This was the moment of truth for me, the unreal reality. I had to wake up from the dream and wake up I did.

A few moments after I arrived in the office, Lucky's wife arrived in Jo'burg from Newcastle where they lived. Instead of coming to the office, we advised that she be taken to their other house in Bruma Lake about fifteen minutes' drive away. We went to the house and found her waiting outside in the car as we had the house keys. We all went inside the house and she sat on the couch and cried; all she could do was cry. I held her as tight as I could and just let her cry. There were no words to comfort her; I had to let her let it out. She had come from Newcastle with one of her sisters, and other family members then joined a few moments later.

We were all confused, not knowing where to start. If it wasn't for the help of the late Tiny Siluma (may his soul rest in eternal peace) who was the only person in his senses, a lot of things could have gone wrong. Pardon me as his death immediately after Lucky is also baffling. He is just another number in the book, he died a death of a bullet also. Oh Lord. Anyway what can we say. Firstly the media was waiting at the gate, phones were ringing left, right and centre – the world wanted the story. None of us had heard the full story. We didn't know what to tell anyone as we, ourselves, didn't know what had happened.

My tears dried the moment I laid my eyes on Lucky's wife. I stopped crying when I looked at Lucky's mother, his sisters and his daughter. I couldn't begin to fathom their loss. Everyone was overcome by emotion and we knew nothing except the unreal reality of the news. My phone wouldn't stop ringing; both local and international media wanted the story, the story none of us could tell. Two of Lucky's children who were with their father when he was murdered were still at the police station undergoing questioning. These were the only two people who could tell the story. How did we then deal with the sometimes irritating media who were so hungry for this story? Having spent time with Lucky and knowing his approach to the media (when the media want a story give them the story), we told them, "the police are investigating the matter". If you try and give information you heard from someone who also heard it from someone you end up being quoted on things you never said in the first place and by the time you read it yourself you know this is not what you said. We had to buy some time because the calls were too much.

I had never met Lucky's family before that day, but I'd got to know all of them through the stories he'd told. If one of his children taught him a new rhyme from crèche he would share it and tell you how they pronounced certain English words; he had so much love for his children. I must mention that he was also overly protective of them; he treated them like they were his jewels. I was fortunate to have met his son Thokozani in 2006 when he started college. Lucky had single-handedly raised his children; first it was Sibongile and then Thokozani. Lucky was reunited with Thokozani when he was about 9 or 10, after struggling to see him and become a part of his life. He understood the pain of growing up without a father and he vowed never to put any child through that in his life. He went on to dedicate a song to his son – "My son, I am Sorry." Sibongile was her father's daughter – the apple of her father's eye. Lucky was very proud of, and committed to, his daughter. I hadn't met Lucky's other daughter, Nonkululeko, the new addition to the family. On one of our trips he mentioned that he had just been introduced to another daughter whom he hadn't known. But he confirmed immediately that if I saw her I would know she was his daughter. He explained how it had happened; the story was painful to him but he vowed to work on the time lost and he tried everything he could to bridge the gap. He had to learn to know his adult daughter and he never once complained that it was difficult. He was going to be a father to her, no matter what the circumstances around her upbringing were. He said, "Rasta, it is painful to me for many reasons that my daughter couldn't enjoy all the benefits my other children enjoyed, but I will make it up to her. It wasn't her fault and neither was it mine that we didn't meet earlier."

The amazing part was that she was also a musician, even before they met. Knowing Lucky he was never going to let his children become musicians, more especially the female ones. He had been in the industry long enough and had seen it all – and I mean all. He knew the struggles of the music industry and wouldn't have wanted any of his offspring to be exposed to those challenges. Unfortunately, her career was already happening so he had no control. Lucky wanted to educate all his children so that they could have better futures and never wanted them to suffer life's hardships. He made sure his children wouldn't lack anything.

There was a time in his life when strange people would claim he

165

was their son. At one time a Zimbabwean family travelled to South Africa to meet him. They claimed Lucky had left Zimbabwe when he was a young boy and that now they had found their son! To his amazement the parents were only a few years older than him and when Lucky asked them if they remembered what their son looked like, they couldn't confirm it. He asked them if he'd looked like him, and they couldn't confirm that either. If you had a son that went missing five years ago do you expect him to have grown a beard this big and have dreadlocks this long? And if you are forty years old and I am thirty would you have given birth to me when you were only ten?

He never discounted that maybe there were a few other Lucky Dubes who ran away from their homes. What was ironic about his story was that he was looking for his biological father, as that was the only thing missing in his life. The rest of his life story was intact. He knew his family including his uncle, aunt whom he adored very much, cousins and extended family. He made jokes about it, saying "I have a dream; my dream is that one day when I am at home a handsome rich guy will come looking for me … when I ask him who he is he'll say "I'm your father". That's my dream, this guy should come and find me and when he comes he should be a rich guy!"

He had tried for years to trace his biological father. It was important for him to find his source of being and from the list of possibilities that he had, he approached a certain Mr Mabuza. He asked the many questions he'd been asking for years; he even had a strategy when approaching these people. The first question was answered correctly, the second correctly and the third correctly. As he ran out of questions the guy confirmed, "I've known that you were my son all along. Please forgive me for not approaching you, I didn't want to complicate my life. I was married and have other children. You are indeed my son".

He was baffled by this and said to this guy, "all this while you have known and never bothered to connect with me? Do you know what

166

I've gone through my whole life trying to look for you?"

He was surprised that his biological father wasn't impressed by the fact that he was famous. He thought this man would be so excited that he'd finally met his famous son, but none of that seemed to move this man. The previous guys were only too happy to go for paternity tests and probably wished the tests would come out positive. Then here was this guy who had known that he had a famous son but none of it moved him or tempted him to go and claim him. It was a trying moment for him. He had to be really sure whether it was indeed the truth. The paternity tests came out positive; Lucky Dube had finally found the missing piece of the puzzle and he felt complete for the first time in his life. It was an emotional exercise, one which was draining, but he confirmed he needed to know who he was. I was touched by his never give up attitude. He was confused by his father's attitude towards him but at the same time humbled to know that this person never once came and claimed him or asked for anything from him. And in fact, his biological father was well off. He felt at ease with this new discovery and he and his father never forced matters on each other. The last I heard about his father was when Lucky invited his father to his wedding. He honored the invitation, and Lucky too, was honored.

After the shockwaves subsided, the late Tiny Siluma called Mandla and me aside and told us to assist the family and guide them. There was confusion in the house as no one knew what the next step should be. He suggested we call Lucky's family and a few relatives for a short meeting, to decide what to do next. To my surprise, I was asked to become the family spokesperson on media-related issues and because no one knew exactly what had happened, the family might find itself being misquoted and misled. The two children were still at the police station with no senior family member present; Lucky's body was at the Hillbrow government mortuary; the family was at his house. Mandla then suggested that Lucky's sister take charge of the situation and advise the family, on a practical level, what the next steps should be. Feeling too emotional, she suggested we help them figure out what should happen next. I remember one of the family members indicating the importance of them driving back to the farm as Sabbath was approaching. Biblically, the Sabbath day is the day of rest.

Lucky always observed the Sabbath day and was a staunch member of the Nazarene under the leadership of Shembe. The Shembe church is a blend of Old Testament-based religion and Zulu social and moral behaviour. Lucky had been recruited into the church by a relative a few years before and was very dedicated to the church and followed their spiritual beliefs. It was through this church that he had found true happiness – the real meaning of life. He had been moving crowds with his songs all along without any spiritual base or guidance. He had now found a spiritual home that made sense to him. A home he had been longing for, for so long, and once he found it, he didn't look back. Through one of his songs Ding Ding Licky Licky Bong from the album The Other Side he confessed he'd made a wrong turn in his life before, and he thanked God for another chance. He didn't blame anyone for his earlier struggles and misfortunes in life. He was making amends since he'd discovered his spiritual home and he was grounded in it, serving his God the best way he could.

So, as the family rushed back to Newcastle, Mandla, myself and daughter Sibongile stayed to wait for Thokozani and Nonkululeko. Thokozani arrived back alone. I can't describe the look on his face. What I can remember is that he kept squatting as if he was too tired to stand up straight. We explained that the rest of the family members had gone to Newcastle. We asked him if he wanted us to take him home but he said he still had to stay in Jo'burg and that he would leave the next morning. I have never wanted to remember the imprint on my mind of this picture, until now that I have to write about it. It was too sad; I can't explain how full of grief the picture was.

I felt too close to the murder scene. I'd endured my mother's death, but this moment was beyond my mind's comprehension, even

168

though I'm a strong-willed and very capable person. My body went into shock mode in a manner I could not grasp. This was an out of body experience so overwhelming there was automatic release of body fluids – I hope you understand. I was tempted to ask Thokozani about what had happened but couldn't bring myself to do it. I had a responsibility to explain to the media the details of Lucky's death, but I really didn't care at that point. How could I be so insensitive and ask Lucky's son such a question? Can't I see he's hurting? I was comfortable with this decision; media or no media, I wasn't ready to talk about Lucky in the past tense. I had to process things in my head first, and in my heart and my spirit. I had a lot of things to process before I could speak about Lucky, the late.

Nonkululeko had gone home to her mother. I stood there not knowing what to say to Thokozani. I couldn't reconcile the fact that he had to go back to where he lived. His father had been shot right at the gate of where he lived. How was he expected to go back there now and live one more day? Mandla and I asked him to stay at the house until the next day, when he could go home to Newcastle. He agreed and we left Thokozani and Sibongile at the house.

I had forgotten that I'd parked my car at the airport when I left for Botswana. Mandla had to take me there to fetch it, and as I drove home on my own, I battled with my demons. I felt my faith and my emotions failing me; my mind was all over the place. I got home to find my children had been waiting, traumatized by the news. They had known Lucky for the past eight years and had interacted with him on many occasions. Each one of them could tell a story about this and that experience with Lucky. I explained to them what had happened and we were all in shock and disbelief. I pretended I was too tired, that I wanted to rest, because the more I looked into these beautiful faces the more it hurt. The information that I gathered during the next few days didn't make sense at all. How could anyone shoot and kill someone for a piece of steel with rubber wheels? Or rather, how could anyone shoot and kill Lucky Dube, for anything? He had bought that car in 2006, the same year I worked on a tour with him in Madagascar. Getting that tour off the

169

ground was very problematic and stressful, but eventually it happened. Dave Jacobs, from the US, who managed Lucky's tours in other territories, had to come to South Africa to join Lucky and the band on this tour. Lucky drove his new car so that he could show it to us, and I remember him telling Dave and me that he had bought a car that could talk! He asked us to go down to the basement to see his new addition. It was a beautiful, latest top of the range Chrysler. He had this personal thing about cars and would give them names. He treated them like human beings – Lucky had respect for everything.

As I've said before, I battle to understand how anyone could kill him for anything. I tried to process information in my head and I searched my heart for information that could help me figure out why he was killed. The man was so peaceful no one wanted to be his enemy; he was a man of honour, integrity – a noble man. He was the same guy who'd just released an album about respect. In the title track, Respect, he sang about love; he declared his love for those who hated him, he blessed even those that cursed him … Lucky would come up with the idea of love out of the blue. "Rasta, can you imagine if everybody loved everybody how beautiful the world would be?" Sometimes he said this tongue in cheek, but at times he would refer to a specific event. I would argue if he was trying to be a fan of Clarence Carter who composed a song about being neighbourly in a naughty way; we would go on and on about the concept of love. But seriously, if you loved your neighbour with the same love that you love yourself, would we have the same issues that we have as a society?

Jesus knew that the benefits of the love concept meant everything. Summing up all the laws in the Bible, He said it is all about love. If you loved your God and loved your neighbour, why would you want to have issues with them if their kids are making a noise, or their dogs are barking all day? Why would you have issues with their irritating music, or their bright lights that disturb you at night? The answer is that when you love your neighbourr your neighbour loves you, so these human issues become easy to deal with. "Okay neighbour, your dog barks and my child is trying to study … can we make a plan?" The neighbour then ensures, in a friendly way, that the dog is taken care of.

Neighbor applies to anyone worthy of God's love. In its simplistic form, if you loved your neighbor you wouldn't harbour ill feelings or thoughts. So murder, covetousness, stealing, rape, and other harmful behaviors would automatically fall away, as no one wants their loved ones to come into harm's way. Lucky was referring to this type of Love when he composed the song Respect.

Throughout his career Lucky was never a person who liked singing other artists' songs. He loved Foreigner's I Wanna Know What Love Is – a song the whole world came to know and that almost became the world anthem. This was one song he couldn't resist; he sang it as if it was his own composition. He loved and embraced the message of love. I once asked why he loved this song so much. "Rasta, people need love, South Africa needs love, and everyone just like me would like to know what love is. If we had love there would be no suffering in the world and there would be no wars in the world."

As I sat in my bedroom trying to recollect the events following his death, I remembered the difficulties we encountered on previous tours. Almost every tour that we'd planned the previous two years had been plagued with difficulties. In August 2007 his US tour was also organized under very difficult circumstances. The work permits were granted very late and as a result of that, appointments for visas couldn't be secured on time. The tour couldn't be cancelled as it had been marketed and advertised aggressively. As a result of that, we had to fly to Cape Town to do the visas there. The US consulate requires everyone to be present when they apply for visas, which meant that the whole band had to be flown to Cape Town.

The visa process was smooth in Cape Town and the visas were issued the same day. While we were waiting for our flight back to Jo'burg at Cape Town International Airport, Lucky told me that it was becoming difficult for him to continue with his work. He referred to what my little daughter had said in 2006. Lucky and the band were on their way to the European tour and on this occasion I took my youngest daughter Kamano, who was then only ten, to the airport with me to check that everything was okay. On our way there she asked me how long Lucky was going for, and I told her about a month. "Mommy, I feel sorry for his children because he's always away on tour," she said. I was amazed that this ten-year-old understood the importance of a present father. On another occasion I took her to Lucky's office and as we parked our car next to his, I mentioned that this car belongs to Lucky. It was his Jaguar. She then exclaimed, "I thought Lucky would drive such cars as Michael Jackson's." She always took me by surprise with her unexpectedly mature comments.

The one thing that caught my attention as Lucky and I discussed these challenges, was the way he responded to them all. As if he knew he was being recalled, he always assured me he knew why all of this was happening. "It's no one's fault, it has to do with me," he said. He never got to explain that point. I sit today and try to connect the dots; he was saying something to me that I didn't understand then. Neither was I prepared to understand it then; it was not for me to understand. Only he and his God understood it.

So, going back once more, I sat in my bedroom trying to collect every piece of information I could to see if there was a sign. I processed information from the past two years; there was no link there. Many things had happened in the past two years, from his band members getting ill on tour to failed tours, but none of this warranted any sign. I spent that night processing stuff from my head to my heart, from my heart to my eyes – my whole physical being was at war. My reality was infuriating. I wished I could sleep but I couldn't as my system was not in sync. I tried to slow down my mind but it told me to piss off – can't you see I'm processing important information? My thoughts were all over the place and I became fearful. My own breath gave me a fright. I couldn't concentrate, I couldn't say my prayers, and I was losing my mind.

My mobile phone never stopped ringing. Some calls were rather emotionally exhausting, some were a relief, and some were just too painful to deal with. I had to deal with all of this.

One of the early morning calls I received was from Nigeria. This guy literally swore at me. "You South Africans, if you didn't like Lucky Dube why didn't you just send him to Nigeria – you idiots!" I just couldn't believe this call; this guy gave it to me unrehearsed; he didn't care how I felt but this is how he felt. He literally swore at me – unprintable abuse that I just had to get used to. I was the family spokesperson, after all.

I received a call from Mandla on the Saturday morning indicating that Lucky's wife had asked that we join the family for a meeting on Sunday at eight in the morning. I hadn't slept the previous night and I felt like a zombie. I needed something to soothe me and decided to drive to the office to be alone. I opened the computer and read all Lucky's recent mails; I tried to make sense of everything, but nothing was adding up. Fortunately, there were people communicating through his email. I suddenly found some comfort in the messages I found there. I printed some of them to take to Newcastle the next day. Some of the messages were personal; people were still communicating as if Lucky himself was going to read his mail. This touched me a lot but I went through the emails anyway. As I was deep into this I could hear someone trying to unlock the door. To my surprise it was Mandla and he wasn't surprised to find me in the office. We sat and chatted, trying to find some answers to this traumatic situation. Mandla reminded me about the meeting the next day. I asked if it was necessary that I go with him, and he answered that Lucky's wife wanted me to – she asked specifically for me. That Saturday night I was able to have a decent sleep, now that my mind was no longer trying to figure out why Lucky was killed. I started thinking a lot about him lying in the government mortuary. How are they handling him? Is Lucky okay in that place? If it hadn't been a weekend I would have asked to see him; maybe I needed confirmation that he was gone and was never coming back. I imagined a lot of things: Lucky being lifeless;

173

whether he was still wearing his hat/cap; whether he was bloodied; if his face was okay; the extent of his injuries; if he looked bad or relaxed. I imagined him without breath, without a smile, without hope, no movement, eyes closed. The last time I'd seen him with his eyes closed was in 2003 when we slept at Heathrow airport en route from Freetown after missing our flight to South Africa. You would never see him sleeping; on the flights everyone would sleep but you wouldn't know if he had slept because when you woke up in the morning you would find him reading his Bible.

He often told me, "you know, these days at church they ask me to preach. It's amazing how people think I can go on stage and do my thing effortlessly ... what people don't understand is that inside me, it's very heavy, I shake all the time. And the worst is at church when I have to preach to 100 people ... my knees would shake terribly." He said he had to read the Bible on his own for better understanding so that when he was called to preach he would know what he was talking about. He said the stage thing was easy any time, because at least you'll have a few fans singing along with you and it won't be that bad. But hey! This preaching thing was different.

I woke up very early the following morning as we had to travel far to make it for the eight o'clock meeting. We left Jo'burg at 4:00 a.m. It was Pat Sibeko, Mandla and I. We arrived a few minutes before 8:00, and the meeting started. I was now up close and personal with Lucky's entire family; his wife, his mom and his sister, whom I had just met the day after the tragedy; his daughter Nonkululeko, whom I was meeting for the first time; and the rest

of the family members, including Lucky's uncle. Lucky's brother Richard Siluma led the meeting as the elder in the Dube family. I had met him in my earlier days at Gallo Record Company; his late mother was Lucky's mother's elder sister, so he would refer to Lucky's mother as aunt. In the African culture if your mothers are sisters you are also brothers or sisters. If your parents were a brother and sister you then became cousins. In this regard he and Lucky are brothers.

I learned through my journey with Lucky that Richard Siluma was, in fact, the one behind Lucky's successful recording career. Not only was Lucky's brother knowledgeable about the business, he also worked in the industry; an advantage for Lucky. He was the one who actually opened the door to Lucky's career. Lucky had been performing to local crowds and that was the only thing he knew, so when his brother told him that he intended to record him and introduce him to the formal side of music, it was unbelievable for him. He became both Lucky's producer and manager; this natural relationship saw the brothers achieving great sales and success after success.

As he was sharing this part of his life story with me, I got to learn that it was at his aunt's home that Lucky was treated with dignity, shown love, and learnt to view life differently. All that he had known in his entire life was suffering and pain. Lucky loved his aunt very much, but I won't dwell on that too much. Apart from close family, Lucky's wife had asked Dudu Khoza, Pat Sibeko,

Mandla Nene and me to be part of this meeting. Things progressed very well – a lot of issues were put on the table for discussion and we dealt with each issue as best we could. I had my pen and writing pad, which I always carried with me, and made notes of important things so that I wouldn't forget and could refer to them for clarity. The meeting took a different turn when we got to the point of how Lucky should be buried.

In 2006 one of Lucky's friends, Jabu Khanyile, died. I remember the day before Jabu's funeral – Lucky called me and asked if I was going to attend. I confirmed that I'd be there, and he asked me to join him and the band in the bus so we could all go together. That morning, as I jumped into the bus with them all, I saw he'd asked Freda Lowe and Antos Stella to join in, too. We were one big, happy family. Mandla was driving the bus and we left for Jabu's funeral. Although Jabu was part of the Shembe church, he hadn't been babtised as a full member. The babtising had to happen before burial on that day. To some of us this was a piece of history in the making as we watched with interest the unknown proceedings. Lucky was part of the babtising and understood the procedure very well.

The events that followed after the babtising of the late Jabu Khanyile infuriated Lucky. He had never been able to attend the entertainment industry funerals before, as he was either on tour abroad or the funerals were held on a Saturday, the Sabbath. This was to be his first experience. He wasn't aware that when an artist dies we celebrate their life the way they lived; artists are celebrated in music. We would sing and dance, with live performances. We didn't plan to join the masses going to the cemetery; we had to drive back. Before the bus could leave, he asked Mandla to turn off the engine. We were all surprised, especially when he stood in the bus facing all of us and told us that what he'd seen that day was a total insult to any human being. He told us that none of the things that were done there should happen at his funeral! To him this was taboo.

As Lucky's brother spoke, I noted the concerns, and once he was done I had to raise this point. I wasn't sure how they would react to this piece of information, but thank goodness everyone agreed with what I had just confirmed.

Lucky's wife was so overcome by emotion, she cried throughout the proceedings. I had just presented the most difficult information and wasn't sure if it would fly with the family. The issue was debated at length and fortunately, because some of the family members were part of the Shembe tradition, issues were cleared immediately. The burial logistics could have become difficult and the more we tried to convince his wife to do certain things a certain way, the more she cried. The issue that made everything so difficult was that we didn't know why Lucky was killed. How do we determine how to conduct the funeral when we don't know whether or not the funeral will end up being a security nightmare and cause

176

other problems?

At this point everyone, including the family and myself, believed that Lucky had been assassinated. There was no doubt that the information, provided by both his children who were with him at the time, showed that this was a premeditated shooting. It also surfaced that these criminals didn't take anything from him. Lucky wasn't given a chance to give them what they wanted; they just created chaos to make it look like a criminal act. My own opinion was that criminals are very smart people – they would have taken the car if they had wanted it. They had all the time in the world to take the car. In fact, I'm sure other criminals are surprised that these morons did what they did. These cars are ordered in advance; people don't take them randomly. It was very strange the way the hijacking developed further. The hijackers drove three times up and down in that area to check if the car was there to take or hijack. And strange that Lucky had already been shot twice when he reversed the car; the third shot was intended to finish him. Why would a criminal administer a third shot unless he was making sure his victim was dead? I won't dwell on it more than I have. The next question is: who would do this, followed by why? Was this done by the enemies of South Africa, or the enemies of human rights? Is this about tarnishing the image of South Africa by targeting someone who is world-renowned, in order to affect the World Cup? Is it the fact that he is a human rights activist in his own right, or is it because of other reasons we might never know? I had a conversation with a renowned South African musician about this and she was surprised that there is a claim that the criminals mistook Lucky for a Nigerian. She said she had encountered a hijacking right at her front gate and that the criminals actually told her "sorry sister, we didn't realize it was you". From this, my own conclusion is that there are certain members of society that criminals would never harm. Why was Lucky murdered?

The family heard so many theories about this shooting that they had to be careful with everything that followed over the next couple of days. They remained intact through this difficult period, as if Lucky himself were there to say "it shall be well with you". There was also the theory that one of the people who knew Lucky was coming to Jo'burg must have been in contact with the criminals to give them information of his whereabouts. Everyone suspected everyone else. The crime situation in South Africa has been blown out of proportion by those who are jealous of our democracy; they'd do anything to discredit and destabilise our country. They realise that we have found out their tricks of blaming tribal factions, third forces, and whatever other tools there are to scare the world from investing in our beautiful country.

I know what Lucky would have said: "My Rasta, God was there, that's just enough information for you to know, these things do happen and when they happen sometimes we do not understand, even the criminals might not understand why they did what they did, but listen my Rasta, "Nna ke tweba e balehang ka slaaguister" (directly translated "I am the rat that runs away with the trapper"), I am a child of the most high God; what was done to me in the dark will come out in the light." That's what he would say – his level of spirituality was deep. He would say "don't worry if you believe in God; you are protected beyond what you can understand as a human being".

Right there at that meeting everyone was suspicious of everyone else; it was a difficult time. Nothing tests us like death, more especially a traumatic death like this one. Lucky had to be buried amid the many conspiracy theories following his death. So the funeral plans were finalized; he was to be buried next to Gogo (his grandmother) whom he adored. The service would be held at the Farmers Hall in Newcastle to accommodate the multitudes who would attend the funeral. I was given the responsibility to champion the project; Dudu Khoza would then be the programme director; Richard Siluma would run with the main family issues of burial; and Mandla would assist with all logistics, including ensuring the transportation of the body from Jo'burg to Newcastle.

We drafted both the memorial service and the funeral programs. We agreed on who, of the family, would speak at the funeral, and so on and so forth. I didn't realize the extent of the responsibility I had been given until we were driving back to Jo'burg late that afternoon. It meant that I must run with the preparations of both the memorial and funeral proceedings, and it was a massive project. I wasn't even family – I just happened to be Lucky's friend and actually just a 'girl from next door'. Besides, a responsibility of this nature required a person with strong qualities, none of which I felt I possessed. This event needed someone who was unemotional, who had a 'you can't push me around' type of attitude. I am a softie and a pleaser, not qualified for that job! But I asked myself who else would do it for this family and, above all, who would do this for Lucky? When he'd told me the story of his life, it was everything I needed to know. I had known him for a little over eight years and he was a private person, but I just happened to be among the very few people he had kept close, and confided in. So I knew exactly what he would have wanted and soon found myself assuming the most difficult role in the whole saga. I stopped being emotional about Lucky that very same moment; I had a project to deliver and my approach to his burial as a project assisted me in focusing my energy. The objective was to give him one of the most memorable send offs South Africa had ever seen in the history of the music industry, amid speculation that he had been assassinated.

His last album, Respect, started playing in my head. All sorts of things went through my mind as we drove back to Jo'burg. I planned my week and everything that needed to be done each day. One thing stuck in my mind – we will bury Lucky with the Respect he deserved. I was almost certain that things would work out as planned and that this would be a straightforward burial.

We had to drive back to Jo'burg with the team that were to transport Lucky's corpse from Jo'burg to Newcastle; this team included his sister and uncle. The drive was more unpleasant now that we were with family; we couldn't reflect on the issues that were raised in Newcastle. We dropped the family at Lucky's house in Bruma, and proceeded home. Mandla had to come back the next morning to take

179

the family to the government mortuary for the release of Lucky's body. Unfortunately, the family had to wait for the post mortem to be done before the mortuary would release it. This meant that the family would only be able to return to Newcastle the following day.

The drive home that evening was filled with how best to approach the events following, and how we would maintain respect throughout. I knew Lucky believed people should be treated with respect irrespective of creed or colour, social standing, political standing or religious beliefs. Give respect to everything that God created. I knew that. The difference between theory and practice, though (I'm deep into this), is that I know the music industry's expectation. I'm certain that half the things we expect would not fly; there is a culture that has to be followed. How does one go about it without creating conflict within the industry itself? I'm soft-natured, so how would I go about talking respect and dignity when the person who said it better was no more? I nevertheless vowed to find a way around it. I remembered a proverb I'd heard: "When we show respect to other living things they respond with respect for us." I was comforted by the fact that he had respected those around him, so it meant that they knew what he stood for.

Respect for other living things is similar to valuing them; you are able to acknowledge their feelings and accept the things they believe in. So I was comfortable that the industry would be cooperative; they knew Lucky. On Monday I went to my office to apply for my annual leave so that I could concentrate on organising Lucky's funeral, which was a full-scale project. I had to pretend that I was organising one of his shows and it had to be perfect. I couldn't be crying when I should be doing some serious "Reggae Business". I took the whole week off from work. Most of my colleagues weren't even aware of my involvement in the life of Lucky Dube until his passing on.

Lucky had never understood how civil servants operated. When I announced to him that I was joining government he teased me about becoming a typical government employee. I felt bad and thought it was a bad thing to work for government. He explained what a typical government employee was, and although I won't share that – I now know. We would argue about it and my defence had always been that the department that I worked for was a section 21 and that we did not necessarily operate like government. Lucky was not against government; his issues with government were a genuine cause – they were honest and they had integrity. Politicians will always be politicians. In one of his songs, War and Crime, he warned about the different struggles that we still have as a society; he warned of tribal and racial discrimination as our new struggles. Only the guys at the top understand what is going on. It is the games that they play.

The songs that Lucky Dube composed were songs that moved the world; now I get to understand why Lucky became an enemy of the then Apartheid regime, and why at the dawn of the new democracy in South Africa he expected things to be different. His messages worked very well for all when it was intended for the old regime, but once he continued composing songs relevant to the present government, he found himself in hot water. His struggle continued as he was sidelined by this new system that he had had so much faith in. You'd better learn fast – you can't fool everyone; the quieter the people are, the more dangerous the situation. Fortunately for Lucky, his musical career was not limited to South African audiences only. Things were happening for him and he was working all over the world. His career was at its peak. When he was outside of South Africa he conscientized the people of the world of the abdominal system of South Africa and the continent as a whole. Lucky was brave and could not be silenced; he took his problems straight to his Jah – his worries, his troubles, his sufferings. He trusted God's promise when He said "come to Me with all your sins and impurities, I am your father, the creator of everything, no problem is too big or too small.' Lucky continued his message nevertheless, knowing he was created by the Almighty and not by man. His supplies didn't come from man but from his God. He didn't put his trust in man; none of us understood his needs – how could we when we don't even understand our own? News that the perpetrators had been apprehended started to spread in the early hours of Monday, 22 October. It was comforting to hear the news, but also worrying because chances of the system saying that it was wrongful arrests was very high. At the time of this information, five people had been arrested; the police had worked very hard to catch the criminals.

I called Gallo Record Company and arranged that we hold a meeting. I also called Antos Stella to come in and assist, as it was only natural that she become part of the project. The meeting went well, and we issued a press statement that day with details of the funeral and memorial service. Gallo Record was to finance both the memorial and the funeral. They made a commitment and told me to let Lucky's family know that it was their contribution and that it would not be deducted from his record sales.

Lucky's lawyer had been overseas when all of this was happening, and we woke up to a new piece of information regarding Lucky's will. He had expressed his wishes on how he should be buried. We had just issued a press statement the previous day, with details, and this piece of information complicated everything. As the lawyer explained the things that were to be done, our plans were completely thrown. Luckily, the memorial service was not affected. Lucky Dube's final wish was that he should be buried at his farm in Ngogo, Newcastle, where his family lived, and that the funeral should be small but dignified. The press statement had to change, but we still had a memorial service planned for the next day.

We tried to plead with Lucky's lawyer to give permission for us to bury him at the local cemetery, but he was adamant. A will is an expression of someone's wish and can't be changed. I tried to persuade Lucky's wife to persuade the lawyer that at the time Lucky made the will he probably thought he would die when he was very old. I thought this piece of information would move the lawyer; in fact I thought that a lot of people would be moved by this powerful thought of mine. I knew Lucky planned his things ahead and he wouldn't have meant it if he had known he would go that soon. I lobbied those around me and the more I tried, the more people wouldn't listen to me. Eventually, I gave up trying and just had to go with the flow.

I personally enjoy working on hectic projects, but nothing prepared me for this one. The phones were ringing left, right and centre and there was confusion all over the place. The team that I was working with was at their best, the type of energy that makes me just want to go on and on. We normalised the situation by issuing another press statement. This time we pleaded with the masses to rather come to the memorial service as the logistics for a mass funeral at the farm would have been a total nightmare. The masses couldn't understand why their hero wouldn't want them to attend his funeral. There was suspicion that this was the family's decision and not Lucky's wish. Information got distorted and the more we gave clarity on the situation, the more complicated things got. We decided there was no more we could do; we would have to wait and see. The memorial service programme was finalized, printed, and ready for the memorial service the next day.

The memorial service was held at a popular venue in Jo'burg called the Bassline, right in the heart of the artistic part of the creative industries of South Africa. We had planned to run it for a maximum of four hours, but ran late by about half an hour. Our running late was the result of the masses outside that were trying to get inside, despite information that the venue was packed to capacity by 9:00 in the morning.

There was no room inside for more people – we had to just close the doors. I ensured that Lucky's family, including his children, were seated properly; the church members sat on the floor and this was such a pleasure because then all the other dignitaries used the available chairs. All protocols observed. Five minutes before the start, I realised I couldn't take it – what have I been doing? am I crazy? oh my God, I wanted to die! I rushed out of the venue, made sure no one saw me, and ran to my car. I started it up and pulled off

– I just needed something to wake me up from this awful nightmare. I must have driven for about ten minutes when I suddenly thought "what am I doing, leaving the memorial?!" I drove right back in. I couldn't reconcile my conscience with the fact that this memorial service that had played like a dream in my mind for the past week was about to become a reality. My lights wanted to switch off; my system didn't approve of it. I had to confront the demon as I walked back in gracefully, and, within minutes, went back to business. We presented one of the most moving, dignified and yet powerful memorial services the entertainment industry in South Africa is yet to see.

The selection of the speakers at the memorial service were limited to people who really knew Lucky Dube. He had few friends but once you were his friend, you assumed that status for life. Speakers included the programme director for the Memorial service, selected friends, politicians and the union. We had to accommodate them as we had to observe the music industry protocol. The programme director did a sterling job and represented what Lucky believed in. Mr Sipho Hotstix Mabuse was also a long-time Lucky Dube friend. As we listened from one speaker to the next, everyone vented their frustrations at government for letting the moral ground slip so much out of cognition. Some complained about government opening the South African borders to foreigners who played a big role in the crimes being committed. Some challenged the government on the reversal of the death sentence. This was an interesting turn of events. I was almost tempted to start composing songs about the turn of events at Lucky's memorial – the things people said! I wonder: if Lucky was still alive, would he have been on Facebook and Twitter? What type of messages would he be posting? I bite my nails on a normal day, and I was expecting to bite them badly on this day, but oh, there was no time to bite nails! I was battling to make sense of this difficult experience.

The memorial service highlights were part of the letters we received from the Presidents of Gabon and Senegal. These messages were sent via the then South African Department of Foreign Affairs, now

184

called the Department of International Relations and Co-operation.

People came in large numbers from near and far; the crowd was overwhelming. It was as if there was a big show on that no one wanted to miss.

Lucky maintained the humble nature that brought him closer to the people that so inspired his music. He toured the world more times over than anyone could dream of and shared stages with names such as Maxi Priest, Sinead O-Connor, Peter Gabriel, Michael Jackson, Seal, Ziggy Marley, Celine Dion, Sting, and many others. He raked in over 20 local and international awards for his music and videos, yet as a person he was unaffected by his success.

The memorial service ended in peace. People drove back home and the family remained for a bite that was prepared at the Bassline. Those that criticised it did so; feedback is good. Sometimes people don't realize that it's important to give feedback – they think they're dampening your morale by criticising you but when you know what your objective is, it does not matter. We didn't have to announce that we would keep it decent but that was it. The team parted and would meet the next day, Thursday 25h October, to continue with the funeral arrangements.

Spirits were high; some of the feedback we received was very positive so we were all fired up. We continued with the next steps, and everything had to be done as quickly as we could. We only had one and a half day to complete the arrangements. We were sitting in Jo'burg planning a funeral that was to happen in Newcastle and we still had to travel to be there on Saturday. The team had this amazing energy and I was inspired. The funeral programwas ready by Friday afternoon and the band was ready to travel to Newcastle. We had planned that the band would perform at the funeral, so Mandla had to prepare the sound and pack it into the truck to get ready on Friday for set up. So this meant that Mandla had to leave a day earlier than the rest of us. Messages of condolences were pouring in, in huge numbers; the world prepared to travel to South

Africa and this began to scare me.

I'd always wondered if Lucky himself knew the impact his music made in the lives of so many people around the world. He would often worry about his fans referring to him as a saviour, or sometimes an African god. He would say that it is a sin for people to give him a status that sacred – he was just your guy from next door.

I know he feared for his life. When we travelled in Africa and didn't have a tour manager, he would ask me to sit on the opposite side of what the security guys had instructed. When I asked him why he would do such a thing, he would say "Rasta, if these guys wanna take me out they know where I am sitting, so this is a disguise." Something always told him that eventually he would be taken out, and I should have asked him why. I was on duty and although I'd be tempted to ask him if he was ready to compromise me instead, I couldn't do that, I had to live with it, it is a very scary thought, you are anxious even before you leave the venue. So I think I should have gone to training with other women in Lusaka because clearly I played a very important role as security. The promoters on the continent were aware of this part of the rider agreement, and wouldn't risk Lucky's security; in fact, I've never seen such security-conscious people as those in Africa.

The morning of the 25th of October was a more relaxed one; it was a Thursday and we had recapped with the planning committee after the memorial service about the processes to follow for the funeral. The main function was to give support to his family in Newcastle. We had agreed to use the memorial service programme as a template for the funeral, so this meant waiting for the family to forward the names of the speakers before we could go to print.

The masses got the message that the funeral would be kept very small and they were disappointed. The band and I left on the morning of the 27th of October and headed to Newcastle to prepare for the following day.

186

I couldn't sleep the previous night as we had to do a dry run of the programme with everyone present – the church, government, family and the Emergency Services of the local municipality – to tighten the running order and avoid incidences. We worked the whole night doing this and to ensure the morning logistics were in place.

As Lucky had requested a traditional sendoff, his coffin was made accordingly, the day before his burial, out of a certain kind of tree. It wasn't the traditional South African coffin. It would be opened for everyone to see his body for the last time; this was done in the early morning of the 28th of October. It was painful to see his lifeless cold face, as if he was simply subdued to silence. It was true he was no more. I looked at him and he was sleeping; he was in deep sleep. I couldn't wake him up, couldn't speak with him – just watched his dark cold face. I wasn't tempted to say even a word – this was the face of a stranger, it was someone I didn'tknow, it wasn't Lucky Dube. I observed with sadness, for a moment, the face that I knew I would never see again – cold or alive. This was the moment of truth. I had known him in life; I had to know him in death. This was it. I closed my eyes for a moment, as if to engrave his new cold picture on my cold heart. I sighed and I released Lucky to go – there was no point in holding on; there was nothing to hold on to. He now belonged to another world, one that I don't understand. With a cold heart I released him.

The males and church elders had started digging his grave a few hours earlier. The church service started early, at seven in the morning. I remember going up and down from the house to the marquee preparing this and that with another colleague Sibongile Nkabinde. We were going past the singing church women when I was hit by a strange feeling. I found myself in the middle of the singing church people and the digging of the grave at the same time … my knees started shaking; I was trembling and my lights switched off. Bongi as she is affectionately known, then helped take me into the house where I was given a dose of sugared water. I couldn't take it. I just couldn't deal with the fact of seeing those men digging a hole; the women sitting flat on the ground and

187

singing sad songs. I was traumatized by this and if I did not faint at this point then it means I am not the fainting type. I have attended close family and relatives' funerals – this experience was new – unexpected. My!

I wished I hadn't agreed to playing this big role; I wished I was just part of the other mourners. So I could duck into some quiet corner and mourn. But I wasn't. I was running the funeral and everyone relied on me. The Master of Ceremonies relied on my strength to be able to run the proceedings; she was in the room with me and the others as my lights went off. I remember her exact words, "Lenah, oh my God, how am I to run the program when you are so weak? I am also weak, oh my God, what are we going to do!" And she said a little prayer asking for God's divine strength. Everyone began to panic but that little prayer acted like the strongest energy supplement. I recharged, picked up, and we ran. Trust prayer to change any situation. The program then started a few moments later. I remember I was wearing my best suit and matching shoes – I had to look the part. I cannot remember what happened to my shoes. And neither do I know what I was thinking wearing my best high heels when I knew my task would be to run up and down dusty and rocky terrain.

In the Shembe tradition, the widow is not supposed to see the mourners, so she was covered in a blanket, but her piercing cries went from the blanket straight into one's heart. I could imagine what was going through her mind and heart – the worst experience a human being could ever face. Her youngest son was only four months old when his dad was murdered. Their marriage was still so young – it had only been six years since they got married. Their life together was at its peak, with three handsome, cute, adorable and interesting boys.

Then there she was, covered in a blanket, burying her husband. I looked at her, I looked at Lucky's mother and family, I looked at the children and my heart just broke into many pieces. But I still had a funeral to run; there was no time for me to scream the way I wanted

188

to. I'm sure if I'd had the time I would have been the loudest. It was the most heart-breaking funeral I have ever attended. Most of us had never attended a home-run funeral so everything that happened was new and the pain unbearable. We had in the midst of the mourners people that had worked with Lucky from the USA, the UK and other parts of the world. I remember Lucky's two most recent tour managers were also there. The Liberian government also sent two representatives, one from the Rastafarian community and one from government.

That morning I had a briefing with the media covering the proceedings. I was requested by the church not to allow the media to cover the actual burial. I asked why and was told that it was a private, divine service, and that it had to be respected as such. I had to relay the message. Media being media, they wanted to cover it; for them this was history in the making. I had to read the riot act before they agreed to respect the request. So my task was to ensure that they didn't cross that line; it was an extra responsibility.

Speakers had their say, but my heart was broken into many pieces when the children spoke, each one of them giving a moving tribute about their dad. I would cry and give an order at the same time – and it worked. Through all of this there was never a moment that I sat down and mourned the death of Lucky. If it wasn't this problem, it was another, and I had to sort everything out.

The family's lights were all off and there had to be someone who could stay bright in the middle of the darkness. Lucky's funeral was the most painful experience anyone could be subjected to. Sometimes it works out better if you're in a church or hall, but experiencing heartbreak and sad songs at the same time is not on. His children walked up and down in the process, not really understanding what was going on, watching the media with cameras right in their own home; it was too sad. The normal process of a funeral on its own is difficult to bear, but just imagine the digging done at home running parallel with the church service.

To date I still speak to myself as if I'm speaking to Lucky about this pain, such intense pain.

The marquee was set close to the kraal just outside the small gate that led to the rest of the farm. The grave was close to this gate and it meant the mourners would just walk a few metres from the marquee to the grave. The burial was limited to only the family, the band and the church.

And suddenly, all hell broke loose. The media created havoc; some of them ran before the mourners to ensure they picked spots from where they could catch a glimpse and cover the proceedings. I had wished this part of the burial could be filmed but you need to respect tradition and family wishes. I was personally not there at this point; I was on the other side trying to get the mourners and media to wait until the burial was done, after which we would give them food and refreshments.

The program continued. Lucky was buried. I didn't see what was happening during the burial. I didn't get a chance to say my final goodbye, and forgive me if I cry – my pain is one that continues years after he was buried. To me it feels now as if I wasn't at Lucky's funeral at all. I hope you understand what I am going through. I've been to the farm several times since the funeral to deal with this pain; all I can see is a heap of soil and I am told that's where he is sleeping. Forgive me if I cry because this is not how I would have liked to send a dear friend off. Although I appear strong for Lucky's family, I realise I will have this hangover for life.

Before he was killed I had signed a live performance contract for a local festival in the East Rand that was supposed to happen on the 28th of October in the afternoon, the same day Lucky was buried. Upon hearing that Lucky had been killed, they asked to cancel the

deal, but I pleaded with them not to do so. They agreed and this meant that after we buried Lucky, the band had to drive back from Newcastle to Jo'burg and perform at the festival. It was a moving

performance – a tribute to a fallen legend – but this performance
was the best thing that could have happened to the band and me
after going through that day's painful experience. It felt as if Lucky
himself were there on stage, just that he could not be seen. The band
just played on. Of course, they stole the moment, and the band
vowed to continue his legacy after that show.

TRAGEDY IN AFRICA (poem)

Yesterday there was tragedy in Africa

And my world stopped spinning

As I suffered another sharp numbing blow

My eyes stopped seeing for a moment

How I wished this was a dream

But how can I dream when I am standing

Yesterday there was tragedy in Africa

As I watched the news

Switching from channel to channel

As if wishing the other channel was wrong

There was no way

I could believe what I was hearing

No way I could believe what I read in the news

Yesterday there was tragedy in Africa

As my emotions started seeking stability

I became a familiar spectator

To my life marred with tragedy,

I became familiar with the numbing blow

The blows that set in my every fibre

192

The sudden blows that always cause

The suffering with which I am familiar

Yesterday there was tragedy in Africa

As I sit and wonder

If one day I will stop living a life

Like a candle in the wind

As I struggle to understand

If there is another way

Another way to avoid this

Maybe an alternative way

Of a life without tragedy

Yesterday there was tragedy in Africa

The tragedy of Africa yesterday

Of war and crime

Of crime and corruption

Of murder and revenge

Of power and status

Of culture and religion

But yesterday there was a different tragedy in Africa

A tragedy of crime in Africa, You said what

You said crime does not pay

Cause somebody told you when you were a little boy

They said what, they said education is the key

Oh yeah I believe education is the key

Yes I believe, I believe

There are educated criminals

In high places too

They commit crime, they cover up

They are riddled with secret shames

In the high places

Yesterday there was a tragedy in Africa

Yesterday there was tragedy in Africa

Tragedy of the crime we couldn't fight

The crime of their secret shames

In high places

That's just the way it is

Tragedy in Africa

10. THE COURT CASE

The days following the slaying of Lucky were very difficult for all of us, his family, his band, and South Africa. The perpetrators had been apprehended, rumours were flying around and a lot of tension was building up. The band and I met to discuss their future. Fortunately, they were prepared to play on despite doubts about how his fans would react to the sound with the main man not being there. It was a difficult time for all of us. The band had to have a name that identified with his sound. It was Dave Segal who came up with the name One People after Lucky's track Different Colours One People. The name had to be communicated to the media, the international partners and concert promoters. A lot of work was done to ensure that people knew about the One People band. The show had to go on.

Then came the court appearances which were very uncomfortable for all of us. We were curious to know why Lucky was murdered and couldn't wait for the hearing. Unfortunately, the casehad to be remanded a few times for this and that reason, but finally was heard in 2009. When it resumed it was clear that the people who were arrested were indeed the people who killed Lucky Dube. I felt sick the first time I went into the courtroom and looked at the three accused trying to hide their faces from the public. I was divided inside; to be looking at these people who seem to think that what they did was a forgivable offence. When I get a feeling like this I know it's time to go to the bathroom. I excused myself and just ran. I came back, looked at them, not knowing what I was expecting. They could have been dinosaurs, or something I'd never seen in my life before. I didn't know 'normal' people could go and do such a terrible thing. If I could have asked to sit where the judge was sitting, I would have done that. I wanted to look right into their eyes to see if they were normal people or if there was something different about them. There was nothing about them that said "danger"; there was nothing about them that said "monster"; there was nothing about them that said "devil"; and there was nothing about them that said "run". These were normal people who were no different from the person sitting next to me.

As we were sitting behind their families we experienced an act which the correctional service staff totally ignored. It scares one when it happens right under the noses of law keepers; you just start shaking from trauma. The families brought with them money, sim cards, and anything else they could smuggle in to make life for the perpetrators comfortable in jail! All of this happens in full view of the public gallery, but you just have to keep quiet. I could hear the little voice saying you are far from living in a South Africa that is free from crime and corruption. I sat in this courtroom unable to concentrate on the proceedings. I sat close to Mandla, who kept giving me information on who pulled the trigger and which one was on the driver's side, etc. My body was in that courtroom but my mind was piecing together the things that had happened on that fateful day. Again, I needed the toilet – I went out.

I kept going back into that courtroom and I realised that none of the information given would dry my tears. I looked at the families of these monsters, and asked myself if they hoped these morons would be released, and if they were released how they would relate to them. I guess they were worried about their own plight if these monsters were sentenced for long periods. They depended on their blood money to survive. I started thinking of Lucky's young sons who had now begun asking when their father would return home or even call them from this heap of soil where they were told their father is sleeping. He is always able to call us when he is overseas but why is he so quiet now? Please can he call us, we don't mind not seeing him but at least let him call us … this breaks my heart.

I felt very uneasy with the whole thing, there were so many people around there; theories, opinions, clashes – I couldn't cope, and decided I would go back to my office and return to the court room closer to sentencing. My staying away from court proceedings became the most stressful time of my life. I couldn't concentrate at work nor could I concentrate at home. I had to go to work and in the evenings ask Mandla to give me an update. I won't dwell on this, it is done and we just have to live with it. I have learnt in my lifetime that most truths eventually come out. I don't have to worry myself about whether or not they were telling the truth; neither would my having a different opinion change the status quo – none of that will bring Lucky back. That's just my opinion. Other people are also entitled to their own opinions. The newspapers reported on it; the court's finding was that they were satisfied beyond reasonable doubt that what they heard was what happened. We were not there, let's take it to Jah. Having walked a mile in Lucky's shoes, however, I will ask this question: why was Lucky murdered? The experience in the court room was like a horror movie, one I would not like to happen to anyone. I met evil, wickedness, right there in the court room. My moment of Dracula.

I MET HIM (poem)

His eyes shine wild with fire

His heart is cold as ice

He talks like a humble son

He walks like a human being

He eats like everybody does

He lives on human blood

He feeds on human flesh

He's got the sweetest words

But his heart is as cold as ice

He is Dracula

Even if you stay away, even if you hide

In the dark corners of the night

He's gonna get you cause

He has eyes everywhere and

He has ears everywhere

He is Dracula

Try and stay away but Dracula

Dracula will still find you

And when Dracula

Finds you, you are

Another number in the book

Dracula lives for eternity

Because Dracula is not human at all

He is my friend during the day

But when the night falls Dracula is not my friend

Dracula has no mercy, no mercy at all

One night fall on October 18th

The Dracula of 2007, showed up

His eyes shining wild with fire

His heart cold as ice

With no mercy toward a son

With no mercy toward a daughter

Dracula him wanna feed

On yet another human blood

Dracula oh Dracula

A' him go lamping the four month old child

A him go lamping the toddler

A him go lamping the wife

A him go lamping the drummer

A him go lamping the guitarist

A him go lamping the voices

A him go lamping the keyboard

A him go lamping the rastaman

A him go lamping rastawoman

A him go lamping the broda from the ada moda

A him go lamping the sistren

A him go lamping Jah people

Dracula why a him go lamping

I and I....

I and I gotta yeta wata me yeye

Causa dem lamp

I and I..

11. REMEMBERING YOU

Your early life may not have been rosy and full of joy, but even though you struggled, at the end you triumphed. Yours is a story of courage, patience and endurance. Your story has never shamed you; instead you inspired millions around the world. Although your loud voice is quiet, the messages are deep and clear. I understand the dangers and the challenges of this journey, but I keep writing. I'm not afraid of the criticism nor of the many challenges I've come across. I know what I know, no one can take the experience from me. My knowing you was special. Writing this book has been so fulfilling – it has been worth every breath I've taken since you passed on. The challenges have been overwhelming, but as you preached, so it shall be, Jah guides.

The many things I miss about you are ever-increasing. I pray to God to fill my days with the things that are meaningful and pleasing to Him. I seem to be playing a tape that runs daily in my mind, no scratch no downtime, it keeps playing … Your music helped a little in the beginning, but I seem to be tired of it. Sometimes I join the boys in wondering when you are coming back. The dream that you are coming back keeps coming back and I ask why. Forgive me, Rasta, if I cry. The many friends we meet along the way, the many friends whom we can never replace. Yours has been a torment, too painful sometimes even to think; no one can ever take your place.

Sometimes I wonder what was going through your mind as the first bullet pierced your flesh, followed by the second and the third. I wonder what thoughts you had as you were trying to escape from your moment. When the lights went off, as you drove the few metres from life. Did you have time to think, even? As I sit and wonder, I'm comforted by your own teachings; you've always pleaded your case with your Almighty God. You've always asked

Him to help us in our troubled world. I am comforted that the God that I serve is merciful, that His mercy far exceeds that of our understanding.

You may be gone but you remain my hero. You represent the best of me. I admire your courage; you did what you could when you could do it. You endured in spite of the unfavourable conditions of your life.

I also ponder on what was going through your mind when you wrote Victims:

I didn't know she was crying

Until now as she turns

To look at me

She said boy o' boy

I said what, she said

Boy o' boy, you bring tears to my eyes

Bob Marley said

How long shall they kill our prophets

While we stand aside and look

But little did he know that

Eventually the enemy

Will stand aside and look

While we slash and kill

Our own brothers

Knowing that already

They are the victims of the situations

Still licking wounds from brutality

Still licking wounds from humiliation

She said these words and the

Wrinkles on her face became

Perfect trails for the tears and she said:

We are the victims everywhere

We've got double trouble every time.

He took me outside in the churchyard

Showed me graves on the ground and said:

There lies a man who fought for equality

There lies a boy who died in the struggle

Can all these heroes die in vain

While we slash and kill our own brothers

Knowing that already

They are the victims of the situations

Still licking wounds from brutality

Still licking wounds from humiliation

I wonder if those who killed you understand that you were a victim of the situation, your upbringing, the poverty, the many struggles you endured through your life. I reflect on whether the person next to your wife notices the tears rolling down her face as she became the victim of the crime situation. Does the person sitting next to your sons realise the permanent pain in their hearts as they became the victims of the crime situation? Does the person next to your daughters know the frustrations they go through as they became victims of the situation, and the person next to your brother and sisters ... how do they feel about losing the only brother they had, as they became the victims of the situation? They will lick their wounds from humiliation as you became the victim of the very circumstances you fought so hard against. Can you die in vain while the crime situation continues to rob our society of our loved ones? Who is my actual enemy? Was the enemy standing aside and watching whilst you were slashed and killed by your own brothers? I realise we have double trouble every time; I look at your grave and say there lies a man who fought against injustice, there lies a true son of the soil, there lies my prophet. It's almost unbelievable that you became another number in the criminal book of our times. I wonder if the world understands how deep are the wounds of your family from the brutal manner in which you were murdered.

Did those criminals who robbed us of you that day, ever hear your song Prisoner? Did their mammas or their daddies or somebody else ever tell them that crime doesn't pay?

Somebody told me about it

When I was still a little boy

He said to me, crime does not pay

He said to me, education is the key yeah

As a little boy I thought I knew

What I was doing – yeah man

204

But today here I am in gaol

I am a prisoner

I looked all around me

But to see nothing

But four grey walls staring at me

D' policeman said to me, son

They don't build no schools anymore

All they'll build will be prisons, prisons

Cause today

I am a prisoner

I asked d' policeman and say

How much must I pay for my freedom?

He said to me, son

They won't build no schools anymore

All they'll build will be prisons, prisons

As I think about the words of Prisoner I try and figure out what is going through the minds of those who killed you when the four grey walls stare back at them day in and day out, knowing they'll never see freedom in their lifetime, knowing that no amount of money can pay for their freedom. I think Prisoner was a prophetic song; one thing confirms the fact, you were a prophet. Your talent was incomparable; you were able to see things beyond what some of us can. I agree – all they'll build will be prisons, prisons …

My own version of Prisoner, influenced by the tracks Soldier and
Prisoner today:

For the money I am a prisoner today, following

the greed of my heart, killing an innocent

man all for the money, I am a prisoner sent

to kill my own brother by the greed of my own

heart, killing an innocent man for the money,

who is gonna cover up every crime I committed

as these four walls stare at me every day.

Which government is gonna cover up the

crimes I committed, I tried to beg for mercy,

the judge would not show me mercy, I followed

the greed of my own heart, pumping bullets

into my own brother, today I am a prisoner,

staring at the four grey walls.

I stand alone staring at these four walls

today, will somebody help cover my crime, man

oh man what am I gonna do, I cannot change the

past and I can't change the future, not a day

goes by without remembering that moment, the

moment I was my own hero following the greed

of my heart

As the first shot went out phaaa, I ordered

the second shot phaa and I ordered another

shot, I knew the third shot will give me the

satisfaction of my mission, I have killed a

man, why my heart why, why did you instruct me

into the life of crime, who is gonna cover up

my crime.

Killing an innocent man, the pride of a

black man, the man who fought for equality,

there he lies in a grave today, I have no

one to fight for my own equality. There lies

a man who fought for the dignity of a black

man, as I stare at these four walls today, I

killed for the money, wasting a life of my

own brother, the whole world is still waiting

for his message, I killed the message for the

money. Oh for the money.

Wherever we are we remember you. We remember the song

Remember Me when you asked your daddy wherever he was to remember you. Today we remember you, not because you left and we know you're never coming back this way, but we still remember you. We remember you even when we don't want to; the taxi next door is playing remember me – how can we forget to remember you? The neighbours are playing remember you; even when we don't want to remember you today, we do. We are reminded to remember you every day. And yes we are remembering you.

What were you musing on when you wrote Don't Cry?

Although you aren't here to say, Every Time I Say I'm Going, I Can

See You Gonna Cry – we cry. We cry, thinking of the thousands of people who won't hear you say Ayobayo or I've Got You Babe again. They also won't hear you say Together as One, or I'm a Slave.

We cry thinking that you're never coming back. We try not to cry but it is difficult.

What type of guy wouldn't tell anyone he loved them? So I would like to take this opportunity to assure those that you loved and couldn't tell when you were still alive, that you loved them. I

208

know how much you loved all of your children; I can write another
book about the stories you told me about each one of them. You
might not have had the nature of telling them you loved them,
but now that you're gone I'm sure they feel how much you loved
them. You might not have thrown birthday parties for them,
but they know that you loved them beyond material things. The
personal stories that you told as if they only happened yesterday,
this showed how much you loved your own.

EPILOGUE

I believe that there are people who are 'soul-mates', even though they aren't necessarily in a close relationship. People we connect with,without any reason at times, Lucky was like an institution, he was open to those that needed guidance and for that reason he became a reliable mentor.

Our belief systems might have differed because of our different upbringings, but there was one thing we had in common – the Love of God. I have followed my limited Sunday school upbringing and have been grounded by it. I got to learn later in life that it was okay to falter and be a normal human being without beating myself up for the mistakes I've made. My journey with Lucky has made me realise that nothing is perfect; to err is human. Without mistakes there would be no lessons learnt. I admit that I have enjoyed God's favour and it has been a great life for me. Knowing that God loves me has been a silent acknowledgement, but now I can shout it out loud.

* * *

His growing up without a male figure in his early life made him want to reconstruct his own life. He sought a group that he could align himself with spiritually. He had a lot to learn about tradition as a black man. He was Swati but didn't mind learning the Zulu culture and its traditions. In the end, that culture represented what he lacked in his life. The one really important, relevant thing I learnt was the lesson that we can survive and tolerate others around us without condemning their different belief systems. We learn the things we need to learn and leave out those things that have no resonance with us. Each one of us has an important part to play in life no matter what our beliefs are. People are born with a purpose; no one is here by mistake. We were all made 'on purpose.'

Observing the way we were created in the first place – our body make up, our skin tones, our languages, our intellect and our gifts – makes us realise that we were made that way for a reason, but we humans spend most of our time trying to figure out irrelevant things. I've done a lot of soul-searching since Lucky passed on. I've looked back and wished I could have approached life differently. But now I know that God intended it to be as it is. Sometimes you don't need people to advise you because there are answers within you already. There are times when you think something is a problem and the minute you say it aloud to someone, you get your answer! Lucky Dube was a good listener. If he wanted to give his opinion he would; sometimes he would ask what you yourself thought you should do about your own matter, which made one think it through. He would never buy friendship with material things. In fact, the only material thing that I got from Lucky, apart from the percentage I earned, was a CD. It had been lying in his office for some time and knowing that I loved gospel music, he gave it to me. He would keep his friendships as clear as possible and loved genuine people who loved him for himself. Only a few people made it into his book of friendship.

I have learned to always be in sync with my God. My morning shower song has changed. My prayer has changed; I have learned that none of my prayers can or will change what God's will in my life is. I know that my prayer can only influence certain things in my life. I understand that none of my vehement instructions to God, telling Him that I want this or that, will ever change His will in my life. I have learned to yield and let go of the things I'm not in control of. That's how I've learned to approach the Bible now. It's my friend. I no longer wait for someone on a Sunday to explain things to me; I go to church to enjoy fellowship with others and to learn about things I don't understand. After each church sermon I read the verses to understand the scriptures and listen to what God wants to tell me. I have also learnt that ministers are only human; they make mistakes too. If they make a scriptural mistake I will accept it and seek Divine clarity. Sometimes the mistakes they make turn out to be useful to others, so I have learned to accept and live beyond that.

My journey with Lucky didn't end the day he was murdered, it is a continuous journey. It's been the most frustrating and difficult journey with its own dynamic challenges. I recently found myself talking to myself about issues that relate to him, but sort of talking with him. It's difficult to explain. Sometimes I feel like calling him and getting his opinion on issues that trouble me. Sometimes letting go is not as simple as it sounds; it is just the way it is. I don't know how many times I've been through the emails we exchanged, not knowing what I'm looking for. But I just find myself doing it over and over again helplessly, and every time this happens, you will see me pace up and down as if I've lost something but, sadly, can't remember what it is.

* * *

I found it surprising how much courage and effort it took for me to gather together all the threads and weave them into the narrative that made Lucky's life story. Believe me, blood, sweat and tears go into such an epic; it's not merely the relating of historical facts; he was such a living, vibrant, iconic man that there aren't enough superlatives to describe him.

But strangely, each time I put pen to paper, I experienced peace that came along with the writing, and the recording of details was a journey for me as well. I seem to be at peace with the reality that is no longer unreal – that he is gone and he had to go, and that his life was shortened by 'dead' people. I no longer struggle to understand why he had to go. I had coffee with the renowned Lebo M, of the Lion King musical and shared with him my intentions of writing this book, at which he confessed, wow Lenah you bring tears to my eyes, I am wondering if there is someone out there, someone with genuine intentions who would want to tell my story when I am gone. Those that know Lebo M will attest to this, he says words that sound obscene whether he is happy or sad, it doesn't matter. I guess this is the influence of growing up in the United States. Sometimes he takes you by surprise thinking you may have said something offensive, but he has this special way of saying it. I took great courage from Lebo's statement. This also reminded me of the day Hilda Tloubatla of Mahotella Queens came into Lucky's office after hearing that I was around. She came in and was excited to see me, she told me she wanted to see me and upon hearing this Lucky came out of his office and told Hilda, stop asking for Lenah, she is mine go and find your own Lenah somewhere, this joke went on for a good ten minutes and I was just sitting there laughing at the two. Hilda claiming I was theirs that Lucky had stolen me from them. Hilda told Lucky they were the first group I had travelled with at some point.

I no longer wonder how his little ones are going to grow up without a father … their father left them a life and valuable guidelines; I am almost certain they'll grow up to be responsible men and women. They should grow up knowing that their father endured some hard times, but so what? He was blessed enough to have been named "Lucky" and if they take time to understand what that name means, they'll know it was ordained that they should be the offspring of such an alive man. Their father was successful in all areas of his life. He lived a fulfilling life, a life of purpose – not a life of showing off. They will grow up knowing that they are original, they have a right to be here, and they don't have to conform to the behaviors of this world.

My spiritual journey with Lucky has helped awaken my spirituality. But it has revealed a strange thing: I have learnt that the things that I reveal to my God are different from the things that I expose to the people around me. I have learned that we seem to be comfortable with letting God see our iniquities rather than display them to our brothers and sisters, simply so that we can conform and not be judged. Why are we comfortable with this? Isn't it sad that our priorities are twisted? We're more concerned about what other people think about us – and in pleasing them – than about what we show God, and the relationship we have with Him. I'm more than happy to be an image of God and walk in His ways, whether that pleases man or not. But I won't act in a way that pleases man but is not pleasing to my God.

We are all failures if we have to measure our 'holiness' in the eyes of God. But we're thinking like humans and leaving out the most important ingredient – Love.

I discovered so many new truths along this journey with Lucky. There were times when I wasn't proud to be what I claimed to be, Christian. I was merely practicing the Christian principles as a moral obligation, and not acting in way I was expected. I look back

and wonder whether those who came before me would ever go to Heaven. Is just believing in Christ being the son of God enough to earn one the ticket to Heaven, or is the passage to eternal heaven secured by us just believing Christ is our Lord and Saviour. If simply believing is security to eternal heaven, does it mean we can do anything we like, even if it were contrary to what God requires us to do and be? Something so important toGod that He Himself had to command for His children to observeand keep sacred as the Sabbath? We found things the way theyare and we are okay with them. These things that are written for us, I have learned through this journey that there are things I say to my God that are between me and Him and are not for the world to hear. I know and understand how important this is. God has been merciful to me, He has been good to me all the time.

Lucky included God in his plans. He always thanked Him for every little achievement, challenge, for the stage, the people around him, and the provisions. If the flight was smooth he thanked God; if immigration was trouble-free, he thanked God; the traffic – you name it – he thanked God. He asked God for good crowds at the festivals. He prayed for calmness and peace at the shows, for he understood that our challenges in life are beyond what the naked eye can see. That which he couldn't see he asked God to deal with.

Lucky's family and friends knew Lucky intimately. He was, however, many things to many people. I hope that my journey with him will assist to fill the gaps you might have missed during your own journeys with him, because only he has lived his life in his own skin. I also hope that you will find it in your hearts to release him. Let him go, he is sleeping; we can only cherish our memories of him. The memories I have of him are a bus load; I am talking about constructive memories. I remember his humour, his strict nature and everything he was. I have really struggled emotionally to accept that he is no longer a part of my life. I feel as if he was supposed to always be here. He has left a big hole that no one will ever be able to fill, and the only way that I can deal with it is through memories, and this book. Maybe it sounds as if I'm the one who is not letting go … I forgive myself for that, what am I supposed to do when I feel empty? I am only human.

ABOUT THE AUTHOR

Born into a Christian family Lenah grew up with her roots
established in Christianity, she is a single mother of three lovely
daughters, Koketso, Puseletso and Kamano. She started her career
as an administrator at the South African Council of Churches an
interdenominational forum and a prominent anti-apartheid
organization during the years of apartheid in South Africa. She
played a role in programs intended for returning activists from exile,
facilitating programs for political detainees and their families,
coordinating programs for the victims of third force activities and
unrests in the hostels and many other human rights activities within
the South African Council of Churches.

She later moved on to work in the music industry and then
government.

Having worked for the Church, the Entertainment Industry and
government Lenah could not resist the urge of telling Lucky Dube's
story. Lucky's words were weapons fighting racial discrimination,

fighting inequality, fighting all sorts of injustice demons in the world, awakening the spiritual and cultural heritage of the people of Africa and yet entertained the world.

She continues Lucky Dube's work of promoting peace and unity through Lucky's band and the many musical messages Lucky left, for Lenah the journey continues....

www.ingramcontent.com/pod-product-compliance
Lightning Source LLC
Chambersburg PA
CBHW061143040426

42445CB00013B/1521